Does California's Welfare Policy Explain the Slower Decline of Its Caseload?

• • •

Thomas E. MaCurdy
David C. Mancuso
Margaret O'Brien-Strain

2002

PUBLIC POLICY INSTITUTE OF CALIFORNIA

Library of Congress Cataloging-in-Publication Data
MaCurdy, Thomas E.
  Does California's welfare policy explain the slower decline
of its caseload? / Thomas E. MaCurdy, David C. Mancuso,
Margaret O'Brien-Strain.
    p. cm.
  Includes bibliographical references.
  ISBN 1-58213-032-9
    1. Public welfare—California. 2. Public welfare—United
States—States. 3. Welfare recipients—California—Statistics.
4. Welfare recipients—United States—States—Statistics.
I. Mancuso, David, 1967– II. O'Brien-Strain, Margaret. III. Title.

  HV98.C3 M32 2001
  362.5'09794—dc21   2001048787

Foreword

After much debate, Congress passed the Personal Responsibility and Work Opportunity Reconciliation Act (PRWORA) in 1996, giving states wide latitude in designing their own welfare policies. Significant caseload reductions ensued nationwide, and debates over what caused those reductions began. As usual, there were at least two sides. One view was that the booming economy of the late 1990s brought about huge reductions that would have taken place without welfare reform. Another view was that time limits and employment requirements encouraged many more people to seek work than had ever been the case before. There were, of course, many nuanced positions in between these extremes.

In 1997, PPIC began to track this seminal change in welfare policy with the publication of Thomas MaCurdy and Margaret O'Brien-Strain's *Who Will Be Affected by Welfare Reform in California?* Since then, PPIC has published six other reports on various dimensions of welfare in California, from the basic skills of welfare recipients to the role of disabled children in fostering family vulnerability and dependency. In this latest addition to that body of work, the authors find that

- California has been able to blend relatively generous benefit levels and eligibility rules with declines in recipiency rates that are comparable to the average for all other states.
- After 1996, the exceptional performance of the economy was not the key factor in explaining the variation in recipiency rates across the five largest states. Rather, that variation was largely due to welfare policy at the state level.
- Had welfare benefits in California been reduced to the national average, the caseload decline would have been even greater.
- Although the state's percentage decline in recipiency rates was lower than the national average, California moved more people

off welfare—almost 1.4 million—than any other state in the nation between January 1996 and June 2000.

Taken together, these findings point to a policy success. The state was able to balance all three sides of the iron triangle of welfare benefits, incentives, and costs. To be sure, benefits could have been more generous, and some families may have suffered without the assurance of regular benefits over a longer period of time. And certainly smaller grants, higher income cutoffs, and tougher sanctions would have brought even greater savings to the state. In general, however, the state's programs worked as they were designed, and few have faulted the overall results.

The story is not over, however. In the event of a recession, which now appears likely, the time limits and cost consequences of such programs as Temporary Aid for Needy Families (TANF) will set family well-being against pressures to balance the state budget. California's policy to cover child-only cases places it in the vanguard of states willing to pick up coverage no longer compensated by federal dollars. The coming months and years will put TANF to yet another test, and this one is likely to be more challenging than the ones it faced in its first five years. But if the immediate past is any measure of the future, the prognosis is encouraging.

David W. Lyon
President and CEO
Public Policy Institute of California

Summary

In the absence of other measures, California's performance on welfare reform is being judged on the decline in its welfare caseload. California ranks 36th out of the 50 states and the District of Columbia in percentage drops in welfare recipiency since the enactment of federal welfare reform legislation. Although the national declines in welfare recipiency rates are unprecedented, California's position in this ranking is not. Between 1989 and 1996, the state's recipiency rate grew by 44 percent, compared to 11 percent in the median state. Before 1996, however, welfare rules were fairly uniform across all states with only limited variations permitted through federally approved waivers. The 1996 welfare reforms gave states enormous flexibility in the design of their welfare programs. As a result, states are now held responsible for their program performance in a way they never were before.

How much control does a state have over the size of the welfare caseload? Clearly, welfare recipiency is related to many factors, such as economic conditions and demographic trends, that are beyond the control of program designers. When caseloads began to drop between 1993 and 1996, the Clinton administration primarily credited the role of federal waivers to welfare regulations that allowed early reforms in certain states. More recent work concluded that the improving economy was responsible for the vast majority of these caseload drops. Is the same true in the postreform period?

This report examines state variation in increases in welfare recipiency rates between 1989 and 1996—the prereform period—and in decreases since 1996—the postreform period—to address two interrelated questions:

- How much of California's relatively low decline in welfare recipiency since 1996 can be attributed to the state's policy choices?

- Do factors such as economic conditions and state policies play the same role in explaining the variation across states before and after welfare reform?

We compare California's performance to that of other states, especially those with high populations and large numbers of immigrants, including New York, Texas, Florida, and Illinois.

In the prereform period, California faced a number of challenges that helped drive up welfare caseloads. It had an unusually severe recession, which precipitated a larger drop and slower recovery of wages for workers at the bottom of the income distribution. It also had high nonmarital birth rates and an extremely high proportion of immigrants legalized under the Immigration Reform and Control Act of 1986 (IRCA)—two demographic trends that place a relatively large population at risk for receiving welfare.[1]

Our analysis assesses little role for differences in state welfare policies in explaining the wide variation in caseload growth seen across states in the 1989–1996 period. Compared to California, for example, Illinois—another state with a large population and a large number of immigrants—experienced an increase in recipiency one-sixth as large as California's. Although Illinois had waivers permitting higher sanctions and termination time limits, these waivers had virtually no effect on the caseloads. In fact, out of six types of waivers granted to states by the federal government, in our empirical analysis only three appeared to have any influence on caseloads: full-family sanctions, termination time limits and reduced exemptions from training and employment programs. However, full-family sanctions and termination time limits are correlated with state variation in recipiency rates in 1989–1992 but not in 1992–1996—the period when the waivers were actually granted. This pattern suggests that waiver policies did not themselves reduce caseloads; instead, much of the correlation between waivers and caseloads is due either to states' reacting to caseload changes with waivers (so the caseload changes lead to waivers instead of the other way around) or to unobserved

---

[1]IRCA legalized undocumented immigrants, making them eligible for welfare benefits after a five-year moratorium.

differences in states that affected both their recipiency rates and their application for waivers. Such a finding leads us to conclude that policy differences across states in the prereform era exerted little if any influence over caseload trends.

Economic and demographic factors, on the other hand, explain much of state variation in changes of recipiency rates in the prereform period, and the combined effect of these variables accounts for the gap between California and other states. We estimate that California's welfare recipiency would have increased by 45 percent of the observed value if, for example, it had Illinois's smaller IRCA population. Had California faced the same economic conditions as Illinois, which saw both its unemployment rates and low-skilled wages improve rather than worsen as in California, California would have had a caseload increase of only one-third its observed value.

Since the adoption of welfare reform, the situation has changed substantially. California's lagging decline in its caseload cannot be blamed on its economy or demographics. Whereas differences in these factors played consequential roles in caseload dynamics before welfare reform, after this event, a state's Temporary Aid for Needy Families (TANF) program became the most crucial item governing how its welfare recipiency rates evolved relative to other regions. State policies differ a great deal in the generosity of their sanction and benefit levels. More severe sanctions, especially full-family sanctions the first time a recipient fails to comply with program requirements, are associated with significant caseload reductions. Less generous benefits, taking into account both the maximum grant and the income cutoff for receiving aid, also lead to large recipiency rate reductions. California is one of the most generous states on both of these dimensions. Illinois, in comparison, is near the middle on both measures. These differences account for an extra 18 percent decline in Illinois's recipiency rate compared to that in California. Adding such a percentage gain to California's performance would bring its caseload drop above the median for all states.

California's decision to be relatively generous in maintaining a safety net for children and in encouraging welfare recipients to work has resulted in a slower reduction in welfare recipiency compared to other states. This is clearly a political choice. Low benefits and severe sanctions reduce caseloads, but we do not yet know the price families pay under these alternative policies. The size of caseload drops alone will not be the final arbiter of success in welfare reform. If California wants to be judged successful in designing new income-support programs, it needs to develop more direct evidence on how its families are faring compared to families elsewhere.

Contents

Figures

Tables

Acknowledgments

The authors gratefully acknowledge supplemental support provided by the Smith-Richardson Foundation, the Donner Foundation, and the National Institutes of Health (grant HD32055-02). Opinions expressed in this paper are those of the authors and do not represent the official position or policy of any agency funding this research.

1. Introduction

Five years after the enactment of the Personal Responsibility and Work Opportunity Reconciliation Act of 1996 (PRWORA), caseload declines have become the most commonly used indicator of a state's success in reforming welfare. Despite the recognition that caseload numbers say little about the economic well-being of current and former welfare recipients, they are easily and consistently measured, allowing comparisons over time and across states. California does not do well by these most commonly used measures of performance. In particular, comparing percentage declines in welfare recipiency,[1] this state ranks 36th out of the 50 states and the District of Columbia. Between 1996 and 2000, California's recipiency rate fell by 43 percent, compared to the median of 50 percent and the maximum of 86 percent. Figure 1.1 shows how California's experience compares to that of other states. Of course, relying on alternative measures of caseload drops can improve California's performance ranking. In absolute terms, California's recipiency rate has fallen more than that of any other state except West Virginia. Figure 1.2 places this aspect of California's experience into context, showing the pattern of level declines in TANF recipiency rates across all states since welfare reform. By moving from 122 cases per 1,000 women to 69, California now has 53 fewer cases per 1,000 women than it had in 1996. Even after this large decline, however, California's recipiency rate in June 2000 ranked third highest among states behind the District of Columbia and Rhode Island, implying that one-quarter of the national caseload resides in California.

---

[1]Throughout this report, recipiency rates are calculated as the number of cash aid cases per 1,000 women aged 15 to 44, a rate that therefore controls for the changes in the population. Before welfare reform, cash aid cases are cases receiving Aid to Families with Dependent Children (AFDC). After welfare reform, these are cases receiving Temporary Assistance for Needy Families (TANF).

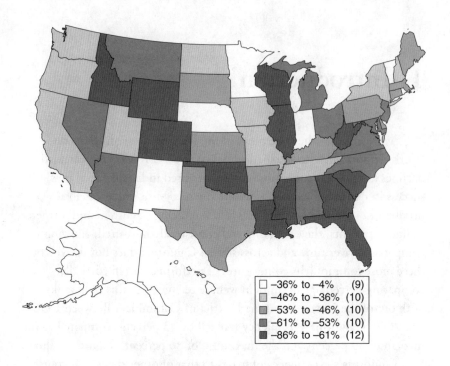

☐	–36% to –4%	(9)
▫	–46% to –36%	(10)
▪	–53% to –46%	(10)
▪	–61% to –53%	(10)
■	–86% to –61%	(12)

**Figure 1.1—Decline in Welfare Recipiency Rate Since Welfare Reform,
1996–1999**

California is obviously not a typical state. Two demographic characteristics in particular distinguish it from many others: the size of its total population and the immigrant share of this population. Both are higher than in any other state. How does California's performance compare to that of other states with large populations and larger numbers of immigrants? To answer this question, this report illustrates many of its major findings by comparing California to four other states that also have a population over 10 million people and at least 900,000 foreign-born residents: New York, Texas, Florida, and Illinois. Inspecting Figure 1.1, it is clear that neither large populations nor large numbers of immigrants are closely linked to recipiency rate declines. New York is the only state of the five to do worse than California, and Texas, Florida, and Illinois all performed above the U.S. median.

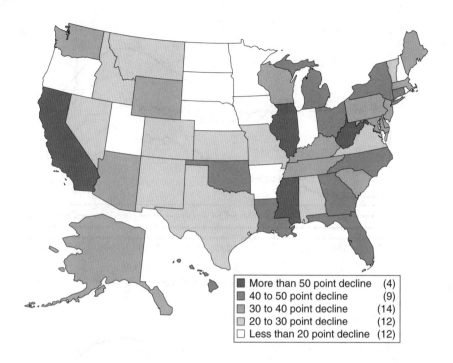

■ More than 50 point decline	(4)
■ 40 to 50 point decline	(9)
■ 30 to 40 point decline	(14)
▨ 20 to 30 point decline	(12)
□ Less than 20 point decline	(12)

Figure 1.2—Change in Welfare Recipiency Rate Since Welfare Reform, 1996–2000

Figure 1.3 shows how welfare recipiency rates have evolved for California, New York, Texas, Florida, and Illinois in the past two decades. Figure 1.4 plots recipiency rates for California and the average for these other states as well as for the rest of the nation. Each rate is shown relative to its 1989 value, which highlights the differences in growth rates. We see from these figures that California's experiences match those of the other states until the mid-1990s, when California's rate pulls ahead. As a group, states with a large share of immigrants always lead the balance of the nation in caseload increases after 1989.

If we look at the individual welfare recipiency rates for these five states during the 1990s, presented in Figure 1.3, we see a great deal of variation across these states throughout the period. For example, California has consistently had the highest recipiency rate, but Florida experienced the greatest percentage growth in that rate early in the 1990s. By 1992, however, Florida's rate began to drop quickly, erasing

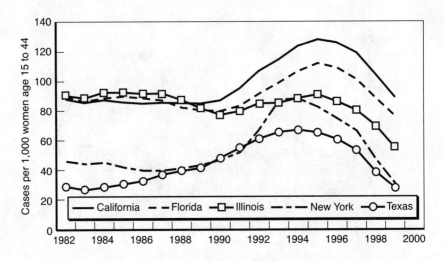

Figure 1.3—Welfare Recipiency Rates, 1982–1999

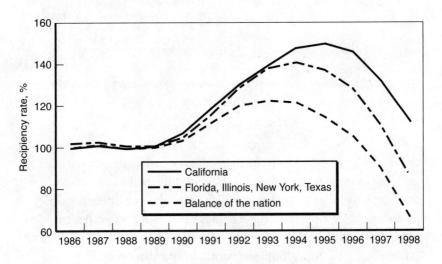

Figure 1.4—Welfare Recipiency Rates Relative to 1989 Level

its earlier growth by 1998. Texas had a similar experience, although it never experienced as high a growth rate. California and New York, on the other hand, had rising recipiency rates through 1994 and turned around only in 1996.

What accounts for these tremendous differences? The current literature focuses on the importance of two basic categories of explanations: economic circumstances and policy differences. The economy-policy tradeoff has been a source of controversy among economists seeking to identify the determinants of national caseload trends, particularly for the caseload decline that began nationally around 1993. Much of the debate was triggered by a 1997 analysis by the Council of Economic Advisors (CEA), claiming that 40 percent of the caseload decline between 1993 and 1996 was explained by overall economic growth, but one-third was explained by the effects of waivers to federal regulations that permitted states to make changes to the AFDC program. The CEA findings have been disputed by a number of researchers who give much greater credit to the economy and far less credit to the waivers. Figlio and Ziliak (1999), for example, reexamined the data for 1993 to 1996 and concluded that the economy accounted for three-fourths of the decline and that waivers had only negligible effects on caseloads.

The effect of waivers on welfare caseloads is critical to the reform debate because waivers represented the first substantial state-level experimentation with welfare program design. Before the introduction of these waivers, welfare rules were consistent across states. Other than the generosity of the maximum grant—which in 1994 ranged from $120 per month in Mississippi to $923 in Alaska—the federal government controlled most aspects of the AFDC program. Around 1992, the U.S. Department of Health and Human Services began granting a growing number of regulatory waivers, allowing individual states to experiment with a variety of reforms, including time limits, work requirements, expanded earnings disregards, and increased sanctions for nonparticipation in welfare-to-work programs.

Following the passage of PRWORA, many of these waiver components were incorporated into newly designed state welfare programs. By replacing AFDC with block grants to states, called TANF, this legislation gave states much more control over welfare program design than was possible under even the most generous waivers. The flipside of this flexibility is greater public scrutiny of state outcomes. Welfare recipiency rates, like program design, are now assumed to be largely under state control, making them the most convenient measure of state performance. The CEA critics believe that the economy, not policy choices, explained most of the prereform variation in state recipiency rates. If they are correct, either the economy is still the main determinant of recipiency rates or the policy changes embodied in post-PRWORA programs have had a much more profound effect on recipiency than any of the state-level policy differences in the prereform era.

This report considers this dilemma by addressing two related questions:

1. How much of California's relatively low percentage decline in welfare recipiency since 1996 can be attributed to the state's policy choices rather than to other factors, especially the economy?
2. Do factors such as the economy and state policies play the same role in explaining the variation across states before and after welfare reform?

Chapter 2 reviews state policy differences before and after the 1996 reforms. Chapter 3 considers trends in other factors deemed relevant for understanding welfare recipiency rates: economic conditions and a variety of demographic characteristics including nonmarital birth rates, immigration status and ethnicity, family composition of the welfare population, and educational attainment of recipients. Chapter 4 describes our analytical approach. Because much of the literature to date has focused on the prereform era, we begin our empirical analysis in Chapter 5 with an examination of the determinants of state differences in welfare recipiency across the 1989–1996 period, comparing these findings to those of other authors. Chapter 6 roughly repeats this analysis for the 1996–2000 period, comparing the role of different factors in the pre- and postreform periods. We offer our conclusions in Chapter 7.

2. Waivers and Reform: The Changing Welfare Landscape of the 1990s

By block-granting welfare funding to the states—and ending the federal entitlement to welfare—the passage of PRWORA opened the door to substantial state variation in the delivery of cash assistance. State-level experimentation did exist before PRWORA, however, in the form of federal waivers to provisions of the Social Security Act covering the AFDC program. Although the federal government had waiver authority starting in 1962, both the number and the nature of waivers granted to the states changed in the 1990s. In this chapter, we outline the variation in state welfare programs that existed before the 1996 reforms and how the reforms changed the welfare policy landscape at the end of the decade. To place California in context, we use the four largest states (New York, Texas, Florida, and Illinois) as a comparison group.

State-Level Policy Differences Before August 1996

Historically, welfare policy was dictated at the federal level, with states controlling little more than the generosity of the maximum aid payment. Of course, a higher maximum grant increased the income cutoff for AFDC receipt, so setting the level of the maximum payment affected the number of families eligible to receive aid. States providing higher grants, therefore, had relatively high recipiency rates. In the 1980s, California's maximum grant was consistently among the five highest, and its recipiency rate was consistently about 38 percent above the average for the rest of the United States. As Table 2.1 shows, the five example states include two of the most generous, one of the least generous, and the median state in a ranking of the maximum benefit for a family of three in 1996.

Table 2.1

Prereform Maximum Benefit Levels

State	Maximum Grant, 1996	Rank
California	$607	4
New York	$606	6
Texas	$197	48
Florida	$318	37
Illinois	$396	26

Starting in the late 1980s and early 1990s, federal waivers introduced an additional source of state variation in the AFDC program. Before that time, the U.S. Department of Health and Human Services rarely granted waivers, and those early waivers each enacted only a few program changes. The number of waivers granted began to increase during the Bush administration and then rose rapidly under Clinton. In 1988, only five states had waivers; by 1996, 40 states had waivers approved, and another six had waivers pending or under development. The average number of program changes per waiver also rose, from two in 1986–1991 to nine in 1996. Whereas the earliest waivers had been granted to allow formal experiments testing alternative program elements for federal policy, by the mid-1990s waivers devolved program authority to the state as innovators for welfare reform (Boehnen and Corbett, 1996).

The CEA (1997) focused on six major categories of waiver provisions. In their simplest form, they can be described as follows:

- **Termination time limits** eliminated benefits to either the entire family or just the adult recipients after a given duration of receiving benefits.
- **Work requirement time limits** provided benefits to adults after the time limit only if they complied with work requirements.
- **Family caps** prevented the grant from increasing (or put restrictions on the additional support) when an additional child was born into an AFDC household.
- **JOBS exemptions** waivers narrowed (or in a few cases expanded) the categories of recipients exempted from participating in the

Job Opportunities and Basic Skills (JOBS) training program, a requirement of the 1988 Family Support Act.

- **JOBS sanctions** waivers increased the penalties for noncompliance with JOBS, typically by imposing full-family sanctions (terminating the grant for all family members).
- **Earnings disregard** waivers allowed families to keep one-third of their earnings rather than having their grant reduced dollar for dollar with additional earnings.

Appendix Table A.1 recreates the CEA list of waiver provisions by state. Table 2.2 lists the types of statewide waivers in our five example states as of August 1996.

California had two major statewide waivers in place by August 1996. It had a waiver to increase the earnings disregard by ending the time limit on the "$30 and a third" rule, which allowed families to keep one-third of their additional earnings. The state also had a waiver requiring that adults participate in community work experience if they received AFDC for 22 out of 24 months. Not included in this table is the state's family cap waiver. This waiver was approved in August 1996 but implemented only as part of the state's TANF program, so it is not counted in the pre-TANF period.

Among our example states, Florida and Illinois also had major waivers in the years leading up to PRWORA. Florida had one of the earliest and most severe termination time limits, limiting AFDC receipt to 24 months out of any 60-month period, starting in 1994. On the other hand, it had an earned income disregard of over 50 percent, similar

Table 2.2

Waivers Granted Before August 1996

State	Termination Time Limits	Work Requirements Time Limits	Family Caps	JOBS Exemptions	JOBS Sanctions	Earnings Disregard
California		Y				Y
New York						
Texas						
Florida	Y					Y
Illinois	Y	Y	Y		Y	Y

to California's under the TANF program. Illinois was one of six states with waivers in at least five of the six CEA categories. These included a two-thirds earnings disregard, a 24-month time limit for recipients with older children, a work requirement after one year, full-family sanctions after the fourth instance of noncooperation, and a family cap.[1]

State-Level Welfare Policies Under PRWORA

The passage of PRWORA fundamentally changed the American welfare system, moving cash welfare assistance from a federal program to a series of state programs partially funded through federal block grants. These block grants have some important strings attached. States must meet a "maintenance of effort" requirement, continuing to fund programs for low-income families at 70 to 80 percent of the level funded under AFDC. TANF still requires that families include a minor child. Benefits paid using federal funds are time-limited, and states must ensure that a sizable share of recipients work or participate in work-related activities.

Nevertheless, PRWORA basically devolves control of welfare to the states. As a result, state TANF regulations now vary on a number of different dimensions, including whether welfare is an entitlement, how income and assets are treated, what family members count in determining eligibility, and what activities for how many hours count as meeting work participation requirements.[2] Perhaps the most important distinctions have to do with the sanction policies, the generosity of benefits, work requirements, and time limits—the same key components that showed up in welfare waivers. Appendix Table A.2 shows our categorization of states on these four dimensions.

Table 2.3, which shows key TANF features for our comparison states, demonstrates much of the range of state policies in the postreform era. California has the third highest maximum grant in the nation and

---

[1]Florida's time limit waiver policy applied in eight counties and Illinois's waivers made statewide program changes.

[2]A detailed listing of state regulations on most major elements of TANF (as well as other assistance programs) is provided through the State Policy Documentation Project at http://www.spdp.org.

Table 2.3

Selected TANF Program Features

State	Maximum Grant[a]	Earnings Limit[b]	Immediate Work Re- quirement	Full-Family Sanction	Lifetime Limit (months)
California	$626	$1,477			60 (adults)
New York	$577	$1,157			60[c]
Texas	$197	$317	Y		60
Florida	$303	$806	Y	Immediate	48
Illinois	$377	$1,131		Eventual	60

[a]For a family of three with no earnings.

[b]For a family of three in 13th month of earnings.

[c]After 60 months, the grant continues but 80 percent becomes a noncash basis.

the highest income cutoff for aid receipt. At the opposite extreme, Texas has the fourth lowest grant and the third lowest income cutoff. Illinois combines a relatively low grant with a generous earnings disregard, creating a high income cutoff. On other features, New York has the lowest penalties for noncompliance and remaining on aid. Like California recipients, New York recipients do not face full-family sanctions. After 60 months, California removes the adults from the grant, but New York continues the grant, although most of it is converted to noncash payments such as rental vouchers. In contrast, Florida has an immediate full-family sanction (Illinois has a milder sanction to start and then escalates to a full-family sanction), and a 48-month lifetime limit on receiving aid.

For simplicity, it is helpful to summarize state policies by grouping states according to their benefit generosity and sanction policies. We define three levels of benefit generosity (see Table 2.4). Low benefit means that a recipient would no longer qualify for benefits if he or she fulfilled the participation requirement by working at a minimum wage for the minimum number of hours. High benefit means that the income cutoff for a family of three is at least $1,000 per month in earnings and the maximum grant is at least $400. Benefits that do not meet the low or the high criteria, such as those in Illinois, are classified as moderate.

Table 2.4

Categorization of TANF Program Parameters

	Program Characteristic	
Classified as:	Sanctions	Benefits
High	Full-family sanction[a] at first instance of noncompliance	Earned income cutoff > $1,000 and maximum benefit > $400 per month
Moderate	Full-family sanction at later instance of noncompliance	Earned income cutoff < $1,000 or maximum benefit < $400 per month
Low	No full-family sanction	Maximum grant < federal minimum wage earnings at minimum hours require to count for federal participation standards

[a]Grant terminated or suspended for all adults and all children in aid unit.

Similarly, we group sanction policies into three categories, where a low sanction state never applies full-family sanctions; a moderate sanction state starts with partial grant sanctions and escalates to termination of the entire family; and a high sanction state applies full-family sanctions immediately.

Table 2.5 assigns all 50 states and the District of Columbia to nine benefit generosity-sanction severity categories. The upper left corner represents the most generous states on these two dimensions; the lower right corner represents the least generous. Our five states fall into four different cells. California and New York are both in the upper left. Florida is a moderate benefit but high sanction state; Texas is a low benefit and low sanction state. Illinois is in the middle on both dimensions. We will return to this categorization in our empirical findings on postreform recipiency rates in Chapter 6.

Summary

To understand how welfare policies affect state performance in reducing welfare recipiency, we need to consider the role of state policy differences both before and after welfare reform. Before the passage of PRWORA, state variation derived from differences in the maximum grant levels and from the application of federal waivers to AFDC regulations. By 1996, most states had at least one waiver in effect,

Table 2.5

Categorization of State TANF Programs by Sanction Policies and Benefit Generosity

Generosity of Benefit	Sanctions		
	Low (14 states and the District of Columbia)	Moderate (22 states)	High (14 states)
High (14 states)	Alaska California Hawaii Maine New Hampshire New York Rhode Island Washington	Oregon Connecticut Massachusetts Utah Vermont	Wisconsin
Moderate (19 states and the District of Columbia)	District of Columbia Indiana Minnesota Montana	Arkansas Illinois Iowa Nevada New Jersey New Mexico North Dakota Pennsylvania South Dakota	Florida Kansas Michigan Nebraska Ohio Oklahoma Virginia
Low (17 states)	Kentucky Missouri Texas	Alabama Arizona Colorado Delaware Georgia Louisiana North Carolina West Virginia	Idaho Maryland Mississippi South Carolina Tennessee Wyoming

waiving federal rules in the areas of time limits, sanctions, exemptions from work and training requirements, family caps, or earnings disregards. These same areas cover many of the important distinctions in state TANF policies since welfare reform, although the states have much more flexibility in how and to whom these policies apply.

3. Demographic and Economic Trends of the 1990s

To understand welfare recipiency patterns during the 1990s, we must recognize that welfare policy was not the only factor changing during this period. The United States experienced a recession in the early 1990s followed by the longest economic expansion of the postwar era. At the same time, significant demographic changes affected the number of families "at risk" of receiving welfare, including unmarried mothers and low-skilled immigrants. In this chapter, we review each of these factors for the periods before and after welfare reform, examining both the national trends and the state-by-state variation. As with the welfare policies described in Chapter 2, we will continue to compare California to the same four states to understand the variation across these states. Data sources and variable constructions for the economic and demographic data are described in Appendix A.

The Economy

The economy has been consistently strong in the postreform period. Between August 1996 and June 2000, for example, unemployment fell from 5.4 percent to 4.0 percent in the United States and from 7.2 percent to 4.9 percent in California (Figure 3.1). This strong economy, however, started well ahead of welfare reform. After two years of economic recession in the early 1990s, U.S. unemployment peaked at 7.4 percent in 1992. At the time of passage of welfare reform, the U.S. economy was in the fourth year of economic recovery. Thus, from a macroeconomic perspective, the important distinction is between the 1989–1992 recession period and the 1993–2000 recovery period.

The national economic picture, however, hides large state-to-state differences. In much of the country, the recession was relatively mild. Figure 3.2 maps the magnitude of the recession by state. The 23 states

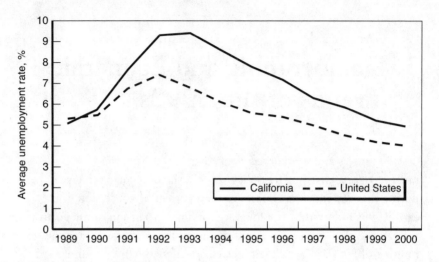

Figure 3.1—Annual Unemployment Rate in California and the United States

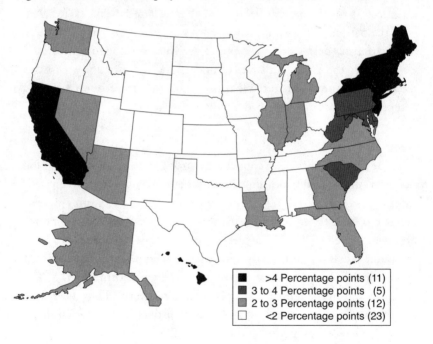

Figure 3.2—Increase in Unemployment from 1989 to Recession Peak

shown in white experienced an unemployment increase of less than two percentage points. Texas falls into this group. Seven of these states, mostly on the Plains, actually had declining unemployment rates. The recession was felt the most strongly in California and the Northeast, where unemployment rates rose by more than four points between 1989 and the recession peak.

Our five comparison states all experienced strong economic recovery. Between 1992 and 1999, all five states had 3 to 4 percentage point declines in unemployment rates. California and New York, which had the most severe and most persistent recessions, had not returned to their 1989 unemployment rates by 1999. The other states had both greater unemployment in 1989 and lower unemployment in 1999. For example, in Texas, the 1989 unemployment rate was 6.7 percent, compared to 4.6 percent in 1999. California's 1999 unemployment rate was 5.2 percent.

To understand welfare recipiency, additional economic measures may also provide valuable information. For example, the wages available to low-skilled workers are an indication of the strength of the job market for former recipients. One strategy to track low-skilled wages is to use the 20th percentile wage. The 20th percentile wage is defined as the wage rate that divides the top 80 percent of workers ranked by wages from the bottom 20 percent of workers. In other words, one-fifth of workers earn less than the 20th percentile wage. Nationally, low wages by this definition declined from 1991 through 1996, then rose sharply from 1996 to 1999, as shown in Figure 3.3. Low-skilled wages in California followed a similar pattern, lagging the national trend with a more pronounced decline in the early 1990s and a smaller rise in the late part of the decade.

Between 1989 and 1999, California and New York were both among a handful of states that experienced real wage declines during this period, suggesting a difficult period for low-skilled workers (see Figure 3.4). Northeastern states also showed wage declines. The job market was only slightly better in Illinois and Florida—two states with less than 3 percent wage growth over the period. Other states fared much better during the 1990s. Low wages rose by 6 percent in Texas. Smaller states, especially in the Midwest, achieved real wage increases of over 10

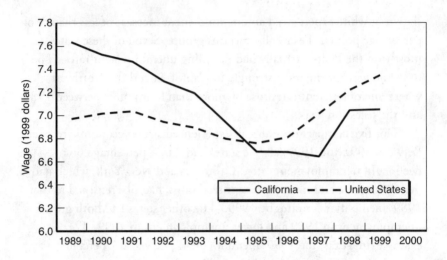

Figure 3.3—20th Percentile Wage

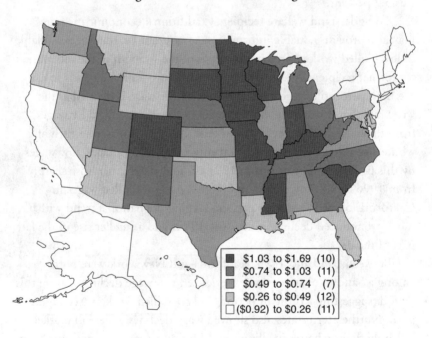

$1.03 to $1.69 (10)
$0.74 to $1.03 (11)
$0.49 to $0.74 (7)
$0.26 to $0.49 (12)
($0.92) to $0.26 (11)

Figure 3.4—Change in 20th Percentile Real Wage, 1989–1999

percent. Our analysis in Chapters 5 and 6 examines the degree to which these differences in low-skilled wage growth explain any of the changes in recipiency rates during the 1990s.

Demographic Trends

In examining California's caseload trends (MaCurdy, Mancuso, and O'Brien-Strain, 2000), we identified two demographic factors that appeared to influence California's welfare recipiency rates: nonmarital births and immigration status as it related to the Immigration Reform and Control Act of 1986 (IRCA). Recognizing that the California experience may not be typical, we examine in this section the relative magnitude of these demographic factors for the country as a whole and for our example states.

The nonmarital birth rate factor is clearly linked to welfare recipiency rates, given that the absence of a parent has traditionally been a criterion for welfare eligibility. As Figure 3.5 illustrates, the nonmarital birth rate in the United States and in California (measured as number of births to unmarried women per 1,000 women aged 15 to 44) was climbing in the early 1990s—the continuation of a trend established

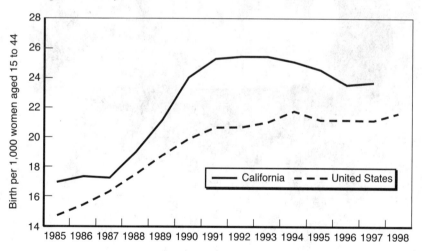

Figure 3.5—Nonmarital Birth Rates, 1985–1998

in the 1980s. The national growth rate slowed significantly in the middle of the decade with small declines in 1995 and 1997, and it actually decreased in California.

A state with more unmarried mothers may expect to have higher welfare recipiency rates all else being equal. At the same time, the availability of welfare may encourage births to unmarried mothers, either by encouraging additional births or discouraging marriage. Therefore, if we see nonmarital birth rates and recipiency rates rising together, it is difficult to assign one as the cause of the other. To capture the role of nonmarital birth rates in driving welfare recipiency rates, rather than the other way around, we will focus on births in the years leading up to our analysis period, rather than contemporaneous births. Thus, our analysis will incorporate nonmarital birth rates for 1985 to 1989 to examine the link between them and welfare recipiency rates after 1989.

Figure 3.6 maps the average annual number of births to unmarried mothers per 1,000 women aged 15 to 44 for 1985 through 1989. States

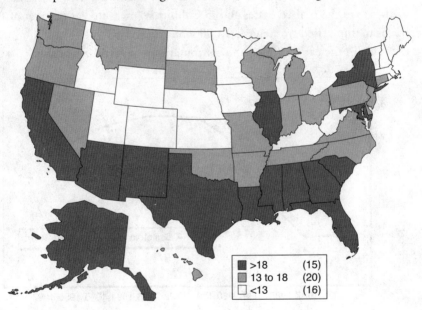

Figure 3.6—Nonmarital Birth Rates, Annual Average, 1985–1989

are divided into three groups: high, medium, and low rates. High rates are a feature common to all five of the largest states. Although high nonmarital birth rates occur across the entire southern tier of states, they are less common outside the South. Other than Illinois and New York, the only places with a nonmarital birth rate above 17 per 1,000 women were the District of Columbia, Maryland, Delaware, and Alaska.

Our earlier results also pointed to IRCA as a major demographic change that may explain the increased recipiency rates in the early 1990s. IRCA legalized 2.7 million undocumented immigrants residing in this country, making these legalized immigrants eligible for welfare after a five-year moratorium on benefits. Immigrants legalized under IRCA were more likely to be poor than immigrants who entered legally, and the legalizations may have encouraged resident immigrants to apply for benefits for their citizen children even if they themselves were barred from aid receipt. IRCA may also have led to additional entries as legalized immigrants brought their families to the United States.

California alone received over half of the immigrants legalized under IRCA—a total of 194 legalized immigrants for every 1,000 women aged 15 to 44 living in California. Although all five comparison states received among the highest per capita numbers of IRCA legalizations, even Texas, the second highest IRCA state, had only half as many legalized immigrants as California.

Besides nonmarital births and IRCA legalizations, a number of other demographic characteristics may indicate the likelihood of cases leaving the rolls. States with particularly hard-to-employ caseloads could experience faster growth and slower decline in welfare recipiency rates in the future. As we discuss in the next chapter, our analysis includes four such measures: the percentage of cases with a child aged 0 to 2, the percentage of cases with three or more children, the percentage of aided adults who are not U.S. citizens, and the percentage of aided adults with 0 to 9 years of schooling. Child care may be a significant barrier to employment for parents of very young children or a large number of children. Adults with little schooling or poor English language skills may be less employable than other adults.

California ranks above the national average on each of these indicators of hard-to-employ cases (see Table 3.1). Linked with the high

Table 3.1

Share of Caseload with Selected Demographic Characteristics

State	Share of AFDC/TANF Caseload with		Share of AFDC/TANF Adults	
	3 or More Children	Children Under Age 2	Noncitizen	0 to 9 Years of School[a]
		1989		
California	27	41	23	
Florida	25	41	10	
Illinois	29	35	2	
New York	26	39	12	
Texas	32	38	7	
National average	25	37	3	
		1996		
California	27	34	32	22
Florida	24	39	11	18
Illinois	29	43	6	10
New York	23	37	21	19
Texas	25	37	14	30
National average	26	35	5	16

NOTE: States ranking in the top five are indicated in boldface.

[a]Years of schooling available for 1998 only.

share of IRCA immigrants, California had the highest share of noncitizen cases in the nation. In 1989, noncitizens headed almost one in four AFDC cases in California. By 1996, this share had increased to nearly one in three. However, California does not rank in the top five states on any of the other measures.

Summary

The welfare waivers and eventual passage of PRWORA occurred against a backdrop of economic and demographic changes that also influenced welfare recipiency during the 1990s. We entered the decade with many more families at risk of receiving welfare, because of rising nonmarital birth rates and the legalization of largely disadvantaged immigrants under IRCA. On the other hand, the recession that opened the decade was followed by the longest economic boom in the postwar period. Still, it took longer for the good economy to be reflected in wage

22

growth at the bottom of the wage distribution: Low-end wages remained below their 1991 levels in 1999 in both California and the United States as a whole.

Table 3.2 summarizes where California stood in comparison with large states in terms of the recession, wage growth, nonmarital birth rates, and IRCA legalizations. On all four measures, California was positioned for higher caseload growth and more difficulty in moving families into employment: The recession was severe, low-skilled wages were falling, nonmarital birth rates were high, and the state's share of IRCA legalizations very high. In contrast, some smaller states fared well on most of these measures, including the states with the largest caseload declines since welfare reform: Wyoming (in percentage terms) and West Virginia (in levels). Both of these states escaped the recession, experienced low nonmarital birth rates, and were relatively unaffected by IRCA.

How much do these economic and demographic factors explain pre- or postreform differences in state performance on welfare recipiency? In the next chapter, we review our methodology in addressing this question.

Table 3.2

Summary of Economic and Demographic Conditions in the Large States

State	Recession	Wage Growth	Nonmarital Birth Rate	IRCA Legalizations
California	Severe	Negative	High	Very High
New York	Severe	Negative	High	Moderate
Texas	Mild	Moderate	High	High
Florida	Moderate	Low	High	High
Illinois	Moderate	Low	High	High

4. Research Approach

Our analysis examines the role of economic, demographic, and policy factors in explaining the differences between state caseload trends. As our basic measure of caseload trends, we use changes in recipiency rates defined, as before, as the number of AFDC/TANF cases per 1,000 women aged 15 to 44. To isolate the effects of the various factors, we rely on multivariate regression analysis. In this chapter, we detail our analytical approach.

Basic Approach: Cross-Section Analyses of the Pre- and Postreform Periods

For the results presented in the following two chapters, we rely on cross-section analyses of recipiency rate changes experienced by the 50 states and the District of Columbia in two different periods: 1989–1996 and 1996–2000. For each state, we compare the recipiency rates in July 1989 to those in August 1996 to construct a measure of the prereform caseload change, expressing this in level and percentage terms. Similarly, we compare state recipiency rates in August 1996 to those in June 2000 (the last month of our data). Using these measures, we employ ordinary least squares regression analysis to estimate the role of different factors in explaining the different state experiences.

This cross-section approach differs from those used by researchers such as Figlio and Ziliak (1999) who create time-series models with complex lag structures. Nevertheless, our technique recognizes the role of dynamic relationships linking economic conditions and caseload trends. A key difference between our approach and the time-series approach is that we focus on the longer-term effects of economic or demographic conditions rather than capturing the shorter-term effects of changes in volatile measures such as unemployment rates. We cannot use this strategy to predict where recipiency rates will be six months from now, but we can use it to explain state-to-state differences in broad trends.

Prereform Variables

To understand changes in state recipiency rates before welfare reform, we use regression analysis to separate the effects of the state policy differences described in Chapter 2 from the economic and demographic trends described in Chapter 3. The specific measures we included are described below, with detailed definitions provided in Appendix A.

Welfare Policy Variables

Our analysis uses seven welfare policy indicators, six of which describe whether a state had welfare waivers in the six major areas identified by the CEA:

- Full-family sanctions,
- Termination time limits,
- Work requirement time limits,
- Changes to earnings disregards,
- Changes to JOBS exemptions,
- Family caps,

as well as

- The change in the real value of the maximum aid payment.

Economic Variables

Our key economic variables are the unemployment rate and low-skilled wage rates. Because changes in unemployment are likely to have delayed effects on welfare recipiency, we compare the average unemployment rate for the period one year before our July 1989 start (the average for August 1988 to July 1989) to the average for the year before the passage of welfare reform (the average unemployment rate for

September 1995 through August 1996).[1] Our measure of the change in low-skilled wages is the difference between the 1996 and 1989 annual estimate of the 20th percentile of the state wage distribution calculated from Current Population Survey data.

Demographic Variables

Our demographic variables are intended to capture both changes in the likelihood that families in a given state will qualify for benefits (other than because of economic conditions) and state differences in the ability of its caseload to move into the workforce. Thus, we include variables that address the demographic characteristics of the AFDC caseload as well as changes in the at-risk population as described in Chapter 3:

- Nonmarital birth rate (averaged for 1985 to 1989),
- Number of IRCA-legalized immigrants (normalized by the female population aged 15 to 44),
- Percentage of AFDC cases with an Asian, black, Hispanic, or Native American head in 1989,
- Percentage of AFDC cases with very young children (aged 0 to 2) in 1989, and
- Percentage of cases with three or more children in 1989.

Postreform Variables

Our analysis of state recipiency rate declines after welfare reform considers a set of variables roughly parallel to those used in the prereform estimation, with timing adjusted to reflect our August 1996 to June 2000 analysis period. In particular, we again use unemployment and low-skilled wages. We also use the same demographic characteristics with the following modifications. First, because preliminary estimations suggested

---

[1]This specification can be thought of as including lagged unemployment rates over the previous 12 months, where the distributed lag structure weights the previous monthly values equally and truncates the lag values at 12 months. In this way, it has direct parallels to the more complicated lag structures used by other authors. We tested alternative periods for averaging the unemployment rate, including the 6-, 12-, 18-, 24-, and 30-month periods before the beginning and end points of our analysis period. Our results were not sensitive to the period chosen.

that any effects of IRCA legalizations on entrance to the caseload had largely died out by 1996, we drop this variable from the later analysis. However, we add another variable to allow for differences in the probability that citizens and noncitizens leave the caseload, including in the estimation the percentage of aided adults who are not U.S. citizens. We also include the percentage of aided adults who have completed less than 10 years of schooling, information not available in the earlier period.[2]

As discussed in Chapter 2, welfare reform allowed much greater flexibility in the design of state programs. This very flexibility makes it difficult to characterize the variation in state policies concisely. We start out with four policy categories:

- High, moderate, or low severity sanction policies,
- High, moderate, or low benefits,
- Immediate work participation required or not, and
- Lifetime time limit on benefits.

The division of sanction and benefit policies follows the formulation described in Chapter 2. We also include an indicator for whether a state is one of the 24 that require immediate adult participation in work activities at the time of enrollment in the TANF program. Federal TANF regulations require work activities within 24 months, but states may choose an earlier time frame. Finally, we group states based on their lifetime limit on welfare receipt. Most set the lifetime limit equal to the federal limit of five years (60 months), but some set their limit for a shorter period, such as Florida's 48-month limit, and a few have no lifetime limit on aid receipt, at least not for children. We also explored including variables measuring the change in the maximum benefit level and the change in the earned income eligibility cutoff from August 1996

---

[2]In 1989 data on state AFDC caseload characteristics, 20 states do not have education data for 80 percent or more of the adults in the sample. By comparison, in the 1998 data, only five states do not have education data for more than half of the adults in their TANF characteristics sample. In contrast to the other demographic variables, we do not have adequate 1996 education data, hence our reliance on the 1998 data. Education data were not available for Delaware, so this state was dropped in specifications that included the education variable. Estimation results were not sensitive to this exclusion.

to March 1999 for a family of three, but preliminary analysis showed that we could exclude these variables when the specification included the high/moderate/low benefit variable.

5. Factors Influencing California's Prereform Recipiency Rate

Between July 1989 and August 1996, U.S. states experienced an average 15 percent increase in welfare recipiency, or 7.5 more cases per 1,000 women aged 15 to 44. The largest increase occurred in the District of Columbia, which gained a stunning 67 percent or 76.3 cases for every 1,000 women. California's 44 percent increase was three times higher than the average. Among the five largest states, the rate increases ranged from a low of 7 percent in Illinois to a high of 51 percent in Florida (Table 5.1). During this same period, however, 17 states actually had caseload declines, with Wisconsin declining 36 percent.

What accounts for these different state performances before welfare reform? In this chapter, we examine how much of the variation can be explained by the economic and demographic differences discussed in Chapter 3 compared to the policy changes, especially welfare waivers, discussed in Chapter 2. We start by considering the differences between 1989 and 1996, but we also break this period into two parts: the recession period of 1989 to 1992 and the welfare waiver period of 1992

Table 5.1

Recipiency Rate Changes in the Largest States, 1989–1996

State	Recipiency Rate		Change	
	1989	1996	Level	Percentage
California	85.4	122.8	37.4	44
New York	79.6	103.9	24.2	30
Texas	45.5	55.8	10.3	23
Florida	45.2	68.3	23.1	51
Illinois	77.2	82.8	5.6	7

to 1996. The discussion in this chapter draws on the regression results included in Appendix B.

1989–1996: Economy and Demographics Explain Recipiency Rate Increases[1]

In the years leading up to welfare reform, California's unusually high recipiency rate increase is largely explained by its poor economy combined with a growing at-risk population. Together, the observed demographic, economic, and policy changes explain nearly three-quarters of the state-to-state variation in recipient rate increases during the early 1990s. The key factors in explaining this variation appear to be unemployment, low-skilled wages, the share of IRCA immigrants, and the maximum benefit level. Once we control for these factors, welfare waivers appear to explain relatively little of the state differences. We discuss each of these findings in turn.

Both of our measures of state economic conditions are closely linked to the welfare recipiency rate changes. Starting with unemployment, we estimate that a one percentage point rise in the unemployment rate over this seven-year period would have increased recipiency rates by nearly 10 percent.[2] Turning to the wage data, it appears that a one dollar decrease in wages at the 20th percentile is associated with a 16 to 18 percent increase in the recipiency rate. To put this into context, California's unemployment rate rose 2.4 percent between 1988–1989 and 1995–1996. Low-skilled wages in this state fell by $0.90.

A larger IRCA population also plays a consequential role in explaining variation in the 1989–1996 trends across states in recipiency rates. Across the 50 states and the District of Columbia, states had an

---

[1]Each regression was estimated for both percentage changes (version "A" of the tables) and level changes (version "B") in recipiency rates. The findings in this section are drawn from Appendix Tables B.1.A and B.1.B.

[2]Our estimate of the role of unemployment is higher than estimates for the national caseload trend based on the time-series models. Unemployment increases that are above the national average may have a particularly strong effect, but this discrepancy may also reflect our focus on the 1991–1992 recession. The time-series models typically incorporate data for the 1981–1982 recession as well; welfare restrictions in 1981 significantly dampened recipiency responses to the unemployment increases during that period.

average of 19.9 legalized immigrants for every 1,000 women aged 15 to 44 in their population. At this average, IRCA immigration increased recipiency rates by about 4 percent. Since California's IRCA population was about 10 times larger than that of the average state, this finding implies that IRCA contributed an increase of 38 percent to California's recipiency rate. These additional cases may or may not represent IRCA immigrants themselves coming onto welfare. The legalizations may have induced other poor immigrants to enter the country or possibly reduced economic opportunities for natives.

California's "baseline" caseload demographics do not help to explain the state's high percentage increase in welfare recipiency in the 1989–1996 period. Take, for example, nonmarital birth rates. When we look at level changes in recipiency rates, the nonmarital birth rate enters as a significant determinant of state differences, but the magnitude of the effect is small. When we look at percentage changes (which weights changes more heavily in states with lower recipiency rates to start with), nonmarital birth rates appear to have little explanatory power. More surprising is the effect of having a caseload with a high proportion of large families. Intuition suggests that large families may have more difficulty leaving aid, so we expected this percentage to contribute to higher recipiency rate increases. However, we find that this factor acted to dampen recipiency rate increases. This effect suggests that California's relatively high share of cases with large families was a slight countervailing factor during the run-up in welfare recipiency in the prereform period. Other baseline demographic characteristics have little effect on the change in recipiency rates seen during this period.

The policy with the clearest effect is changes in the maximum benefit level. By our estimates, a $100 decrease in the real value of the maximum grant would reduce the welfare recipiency rate by 21 percent. In general, maximum benefit levels fell during this period—the average decline was $56—tending to offset other factors that increased recipiency rates. Although this finding is consistent with economic principles— more families become eligible and welfare becomes more attractive as the benefit level rises—as we note below, it does not hold for the entire period.

The estimated effects of waivers are more difficult to interpret. We eliminated the waivers that seemed to have the least explanatory power, leaving full-family sanctions, termination time limits, and JOBS exemptions. Taken together, these three waivers appear to have affected recipiency rates, although individually none of them had large enough effects to be considered statistically significant.[3] Because all three place restrictions on receiving assistance and make it easier for families to lose benefits, we would expect all three of these types of waivers to reduce caseloads. However, we find that termination time limits appear to increase recipiency rates, although the other two seem to reduce recipiency. We explore the reasons for this unexpected difference in the next section.

Subperiod Findings Discount the Role of Policy

We can better understand the dynamics behind the 1989–1996 findings by breaking the period into two parts. There are four reasons for this. First, between 1989 and 1996, welfare recipiency nationally rose through 1994 and then turned around. Second, the early years of this period encompass a significant economic recession, with a period of recovery in the later years. Third, most of the welfare waivers were granted after 1992, so their effects should show up only in the second half of the period. Finally, the CEA report, and its critics, focused on the 1993–1996 period. Because of these considerations, we reestimated our models for two subperiods: July 1989 to August 1992 and August 1992 to August 1996.

The difference in these two periods shows up in the level and percentage changes in recipiency rates for the five largest states, shown in Table 5.2. Unlike the earlier period, three out of the five states

---

[3]More specifically, we performed the F-test for exclusion of the work requirement time limit, earnings disregard, and family cap waiver variables and could not reject the null hypothesis. The remaining three waivers (full-family sanctions, termination time limits, and JOBS exemptions) have coefficient estimates of roughly similar magnitude, each on the boundary of statistical significance, barely or not quite meeting traditional tests for rejecting the hypothesis that the coefficients are equal to zero. Yet F-tests show we *can* reject the hypothesis that all three are equal to zero.

Table 5.2

Recipiency Rate Changes, 1989–1992 and 1992–1996 Subperiods

| | | | | Change in Recipiency Rates | | | |
| | Recipiency Rate | | | 1989–1992 | | 1992–1996 | |
State	1989	1992	1996	Level	Percentage	Level	Percentage
California	85.4	113.5	122.8	28.2	33	8.9	8
New York	79.6	95.6	103.9	16.0	20	7.4	8
Texas	45.5	64.7	55.8	19.2	42	–9.3	–14
Florida	45.2	87.7	68.3	42.5	94	–19.4	–22
Illinois	77.2	85.1	82.8	7.9	10	–2.1	–2

experienced recipiency rate declines in the 1992–1996 period. California and New York, however, continued to experience increases.

The most striking finding when we look at these subperiods is the result on the estimated effects of AFDC waivers: Both full-family sanctions and termination time limits are statistically significant in the early period, but not in the later period.[4] This is surprising because these waivers were generally not implemented before 1992. If the waivers genuinely reduced recipiency rates, we would expect these variables to have no explanatory power in the first period (when they were not in place) and have greater explanatory power in the second period than across the entire 1989–1996 period. In fact, we found the opposite, suggesting that the correlation between waivers and recipiency rates actually reflects the effects of earlier reforms in states that were later granted these waivers, or perhaps more likely, suggests that the caseload dynamics prompted states to apply for these waivers, a reverse causality from what we had previously assumed. These alternatives may also explain why the termination time limits appeared to increase recipiency, rather than decrease it, as expected. It may be that states with large percentage caseload increases were more likely to seek time limit waivers. For the 1992–1996 period, we find that none of the waivers mattered for caseload trends.

---

[4]Regression results for the 1989–1992 period are presented in Appendix Tables B.2.A. and B.2.B. Results for 1992–1996 are presented in Appendix Tables B.3.A and B.3.B.

The subperiod analysis also tempers our conclusions on maximum benefit levels. Changes in the real benefit levels appear to have strong effects in the 1989–1992 period, showing the same magnitude as for the period overall. However, no such relationship holds for the 1992–1996 period, where changes in the maximum benefit level show no link to changes in recipiency rates. This inconsistency suggests that the effect of the real benefit level is overstated in the full prereform period findings reported above.

The strong effects of the economy hold up in the subperiod analysis, but findings on the demographic variables are weakened if we look only at these shorter periods. When we drop the waivers from the regression for the early period, we continue to find large and significant correlations between welfare recipiency and changes in unemployment and wages, although the IRCA variable no longer shows a clear link with recipiency increases. Similarly, both economic factors—changes in unemployment and low wages—are strongly linked to the variations in state recipiency rates between 1992 and 1996, but neither the IRCA population nor the nonmarital birth rate helps explain these variations.[5]

Explaining California's Recipiency Rate Increase

How can we use these findings to explain the change in California's welfare recipiency rate between 1989 and 1996? The regression results allow us to calculate how much of the increase in California's recipiency rate is explained by each of our demographic, economic, and policy factors.

To understand the role of these factors, we compare California to Illinois. Illinois is a valuable comparison case because, like California, it has a large population and a large share of immigrants. However, Illinois's recipiency rate increased only 7 percent between 1989 and 1996, whereas California's increased 44 percent.

As Table 5.3 shows, these two states experienced substantially different economic, demographic, and policy conditions. California's unemployment rate in 1996 remained well above—and real wages at the

---

[5]For the 1992–1996 period, we use the birth rate averaged for 1988 to 1992, when birth rates were higher than the 1985–1989 average.

Table 5.3

Comparison of Key Explanatory Factors for California, Illinois, and the Average State, 1989–1996

Variable	California	Illinois	Average State
Unemployment rate	2.37	−0.79	0.06
Low wages	−$0.90	$0.06	−$0.14
Nonmarital birth rate (average 1985–1989)	18.4	19.6	15.7
IRCA rate	193.7	54.2	19.9
Percentage with 3 or more children (FFY 1989)	26.5	29.1	24.6
Maximum benefit level	−$219.74	−$26.52	−$51.70
Waiver: full-family sanctions	No	Yes	N/A
Time limits	No	Yes	N/A
JOBS exemptions	No	No	N/A

20th percentile remained well below—their 1989 level. By contrast, Illinois experienced modest improvement over the period in both economic measures. Although the two states had similar baseline nonmarital birth rates, California experienced a much higher rate of IRCA immigration. Although California cut real benefit levels much more sharply, Illinois implemented two of the three key types of waivers (full-family sanctions and time limits).

Figure 5.1 illustrates how California's recipiency rate would have changed if the state's experiences had been more like those of Illinois in 1989–1992 and in 1992–1996.[6] The left-most bar in Figure 5.1 shows the actual increase in California's recipiency rate. The next three bars show what California's increase would have been if it had (1) the same

---

[6]We use the regression estimates from the two prereform subperiods, rather than the results for the full period. As noted above, the full-period results appear to overestimate the effects of the real benefit levels. The subperiod estimates imply more plausible effects for benefit levels: The 1989–1996 model estimates that California's $220 reduction in real benefit levels induced a 45 percent reduction in the caseload. The two subperiod estimates predict merely a 16 percent decline. Despite our concerns about the direction of the causal relationship between waiver policies and recipiency rate changes, we do include the waiver estimates in this comparison. However, because Illinois implemented waiver policies that had offsetting effects in each time period, the simulations are essentially unaffected by the inclusion of these variables.

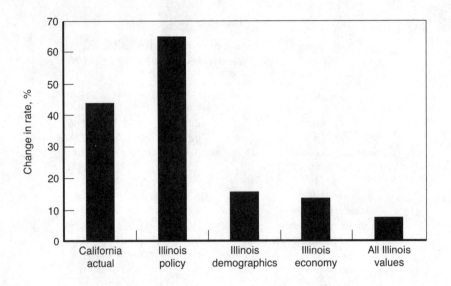

Figure 5.1—Estimated Recipiency Rate Growth in California Under Alternative Assumptions

welfare policy changes as Illinois, or (2) the same demographics as Illinois, or (3) the same economic conditions. By examining how the column height changes as we switch from California to Illinois values, we can understand the contribution of policy, demographics and the economy. The last bar indicates that, if California had faced the same conditions along all three dimensions during this period, its recipiency rate would have increased by only 8 percent instead of 44 percent. (The percentage change would not have fallen all the way to Illinois's 7 percent because Illinois had lower growth than predicted by the model.)

The most critical finding is that none of California's higher recipiency rate increase relative to that of Illinois is due to its welfare policy. In fact, these results imply that California's rate would have increased by an additional 21 percentage points if the state had instituted the same welfare policies as Illinois. That is, the recipiency rate would have increased substantially more if California had not cut its grant level by $219 in real terms over this seven-year period. Illinois slightly increased its nominal grant amount, although not by enough to keep up with inflation. Illinois's waivers did little to hold down its recipiency rate: The waivers together slightly *increase* the estimated percentage change in the recipiency rate, because the estimated effect of the termination time limits is larger in magnitude and of opposite sign to the effect of full-family sanctions.

The demographic variables tell a different story. If California had Illinois's smaller IRCA population and larger proportion of cases with three or more children, its recipiency rate change would have been about 28 percentage points lower than it actually was—more than enough to offset the predicted increase from adopting Illinois's grant level and waiver policies. If California had the same policy changes and the same demographic circumstances as Illinois, its recipiency rate increase would have been 37 percent instead of 44 percent (the sum of an extra 21 percent from policy minus a 28 percent decrease from demographics).

Compared to the demographic variables, economic conditions explain a somewhat greater share of the difference between Illinois and California in this period. If California had Illinois's declining unemployment rate and increasing real low-end wages, its recipiency rate would have increased by only 14 percent. This figure assumes, of course, that the state would have instituted the same grant cuts, which it was not likely to have done without the pressure of the poor economy and rapidly rising recipiency rates.

Comparison with Earlier Findings

Because we are only examining the determinants of the state variation in recipiency rate changes rather than trying to build a model that explains the national trends, we are asking a somewhat different question than the one posed in much of the economics literature on caseload changes in the 1990s. Nevertheless, these findings are consistent with much of that work.

Starting with the increases of the early 1990s, the Lewin Group (1997) examined determinants of caseload growth (using time-series regressions) on data from 1979 to 1994. Their results include specific simulations for California, where they report a much stronger contribution of labor market variables to caseload growth in the state relative to that in the nation, because of California's deeper and longer recession. They also found a significant role for IRCA.

In the wake of the 1997 CEA report, a number of articles focused specifically on the role of waivers compared to other factors. In a 1999 update, the CEA backed off its original assignment of one-third of the caseload decline resulting from waivers. Its revised estimate is 12 to 15 percent. However, Blank (1997), a member of the CEA in 1997, notes that caseload declines are correlated with waivers but more than half of the apparent effect precedes implementation. She also finds that recent immigrants and a rise in the number of families headed by single women help explain the increase in caseloads in the early 1990s. A later paper extending the data to 1996 (Blank and Wallace, 1999) still finds program effects but again finds bigger effects for the economy. The authors report that a 1 percent increase in unemployment increases caseloads by 6 percent. Finally, as noted above, Figlio and Ziliak (1999) reassess the original CEA findings, developing a time-series model for 1987 to 1996 with multiple period lags in both recipiency rates and unemployment rates. They conclude that three-fourths of the 1993–1996 declines are due to the macroeconomy, with only negligible waiver effects. Unlike the CEA, they do not include benefit levels, although they report that this exclusion does not affect the results.

Summary

Between 1989 and 1996, California's recipiency rate rose by 37.4 cases per 1,000 women aged 15 to 44. This increase was more than six times greater than the rise in Illinois, another large, high-immigrant state. According to our estimates, none of this difference can be attributed to differences in the welfare policies of the two states. In fact, California's increase would have been much larger if it had not decreased real benefit levels. Furthermore, if California had experienced Illinois's economic conditions, it would have had a caseload increase of only 14 percent. Our estimates suggest that California's higher-than-average unemployment rate increase pushed our recipiency rate up 14 percent, and our larger-than-average wage loss for low-wage workers increased recipiency by 16 percent. Finally, California's huge number of IRCA legalized immigrants appeared to have a significant effect on welfare use, increasing recipiency by 30 percent more than a state receiving the average share of IRCA immigrants.

Although three out of the six types of waivers appear correlated with recipiency rates over the 1989–1996 period, two are correlated with recipiency in the 1989–1992 period, but not in the 1992–1996 period, which is when most waivers were implemented. This pattern suggests that either recipiency rate changes led states to seek waivers or that states that sought waivers had other circumstances that affected their recipiency rates.

6. Understanding California's Performance in the Postreform Era

California's unusually high increase in welfare recipiency in the prereform era was largely due to factors outside the control of state policymakers. In fact, the major policy choice that appears to have mattered was cutting grant levels, which held down the state's recipiency rate. With the passage of PRWORA, states now have much greater flexibility in determining welfare policies. California has experienced a very large decrease in recipiency rates, but in part because of its high recipiency going into the reform era, this decrease translates into a relatively small percentage reduction. Among states with large populations and large shares of immigrants, only New York has had a smaller percentage decline in caseloads (Table 6.1).

In this postreform era, do welfare policies play a larger role in explaining variation between California and other states in recipiency rate changes? Our regression analysis examines the determinants of recipiency rate changes between August 1996 and June 2000 (the last

Table 6.1

Recipiency Rate Changes, 1996–2000

State	Recipiency Rate		Change	
	August 1996	June 2000	Level	Percentage
California	122.8	69.5	−52.9	−43
New York	103.0	61.0	−42.0	−40
Texas	55.5	27.9	−27.6	−50
Florida	68.4	20.3	−48.1	−70
Illinois	83.0	31.4	−51.6	−62

period of our data).[1] We primarily focus on explaining differences in the percentage changes, although where appropriate we also consider explanations for differences in level changes in recipiency rates over this period. The complete regression findings are included as Tables B.4.A through B.5.B in Appendix B.

1996–2000: Strong Sanctions and Low Benefits Lower Recipiency Rates

Welfare program design plays an important role in explaining why some states have experienced large percentage declines in recipiency rates. Using our definitions of high, moderate, and low sanctions and benefits, we saw above that California's TANF program is categorized as high benefit, low sanction. Our analysis permits us to predict how much larger the percentage recipiency rate declines would have been if California had selected a different sanction or benefit strategy. Most notably, states that impose immediate full-family sanctions and have low benefits reduced recipiency by 36 more percentage points relative to high benefit states that never impose full-family sanctions, as shown in the bottom right box of Table 6.2. These results imply that California might have decreased its recipiency by 79 percent instead of 43 percent had it imposed these more severe policies.

In fact, as Table 6.2 shows, every alternative policy combination is associated with greater recipiency reductions, although only those in boldface are statistically significant. Compared to California's strategy, states with high sanctions reduced recipiency by 26 to 37 percentage points. The high benefit, high sanction policy that had the greatest effect compared to California's policies actually applies to Wisconsin only, so it is difficult to generalize from this result. However, moderate sanctions combined with low benefits had similar effects, reducing recipiency by an additional 31 percentage points. Even moderate sanctions alone—

---

[1]We also tried alternative starting dates for the beginning of the TANF period such as various times in 1997 rather than in the summer of 1996, with results essentially identical to the findings reported here. According to DHHS, 24 states implemented their TANF programs in 1996, and 24 additional states implemented by July 1, 1997. Only California (January 1, 1998), New York (November 1, 1997), and Wisconsin (September 1, 1997) implemented later.

Table 6.2

Additional Percentage Decline in Recipiency Rates from
Increasing Sanctions or Decreasing Benefits

	Sanction		
Benefit	Low (14 states and the District of Columbia)	Moderate (22 states)	High (14 states)
High (14 states)	—	9	37
Moderate (19 states and the District of Columbia)	2	18	26
Low (17 states)	15	31	36

NOTE: Boldface indicates that the difference is statistically significant at 95 percent confidence.

associated with a 9 percent reduction in recipiency—would move California just above the national median.

The estimated effects of sanction policies should not be surprising, given that full-family sanctions remove families from the welfare rolls even (or especially) in the absence of any behavioral changes. For example, DHHS statistics indicate that in federal fiscal year 1998, 30 percent of caseload exits in Florida (a high sanction state in our classification) were closed because of full-family sanctions. Several other high sanction states had comparable rates of closure because of sanctions in 1998.[2] Thus, the available data on state sanction rates under TANF are consistent with the magnitude of the sanction effects we identify in Table 6.2 (and Appendix Tables B.5.A and B.5.B).[3]

Like high sanctions, much of the effect of low benefits is also mechanical rather than behavioral. To see why being a low benefit state results in substantial caseload reductions, compare California with Texas, as in Table 6.3. Although both states implemented lenient TANF sanction policies, they have very different policies with respect to benefit levels and earned income disregards. A California family can earn up to

---

[2]U.S. Department of Health and Human Services (1999), Table 9-31.

[3]Furthermore, the timing of breaks in state caseload trends and the time of TANF program implementation, in particular for the four states with the largest percentage decline in recipiency (Wisconsin, Idaho, Wyoming, and West Virginia), point to the importance of TANF policies in driving caseload trends in the TANF era.

Table 6.3

Recipiency Rate Declines, Earnings Cutoff, and Share of Recipients with Earnings, California and Texas

	Percentage Decline in Rate, August 1996 to June 2000	Monthly Earnings Cutoff, Family of 3, March 1999	Percentage of Adult Recipients with Earnings, FFY 1999
California	–43	$1,589	41
Texas	–50	$308	5

$1,589 a month without losing TANF benefits (middle column of Table 6.3), but a Texas family loses benefits if its earnings exceed $308 a month, based on each state's earned income cutoff after six months with earnings for a family of three. In other words, a family would have to work 40 hours per week at $9.25 per hour to lose TANF income eligibility in California. The same family in Texas would lose TANF eligibility working just 14 hours per week at $5.15 per hour (the federal minimum wage in June 2000). With the highs earned income cutoff, 41 percent of aided adults in California had earnings in FFY 1999. By contrast, the cutoff is so low in Texas that only 5 percent of aided adults had earnings in FFY 1999. At the same time, Texas has experienced a greater percentage decline in recipiency under TANF than California (50 percent versus 43 percent).

As this comparison suggests, moving recipients from welfare to work results almost entirely in caseload reductions in low benefit states but results in a mix of caseload reductions and increases in the proportion of working recipients in high benefit states. Since all state TANF programs now emphasize "work first," low benefit states have an automatic advantage over high benefit states in reducing welfare recipiency. On the flip side, looking across the groups of high, moderate, and low benefit states, we find a consistent relationship between benefit levels and the share of recipients with earnings. The higher the benefit level, the greater the proportion of aided adults in unsubsidized employment (Figure 6.1): 15 percent of aided adults in low benefit states are involved in unsubsidized employment, compared to 28 percent in moderate

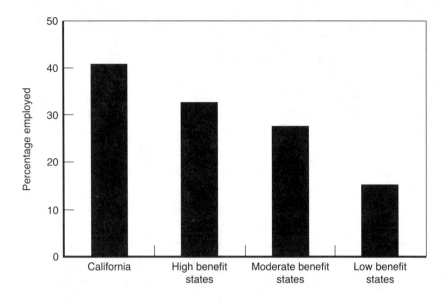

Figure 6.1—Percentage of Aided Adults in Unsubsidized Employment, FFY 1999

benefit states, 33 percent in all high benefit states, and 41 percent in California.[4]

The Economy and Demographics Explain Little Postreform State Variation

In the post-TANF era, economic factors—which were key in explaining pre-TANF differences—are much weaker in explaining state differences in recipiency rate declines, whether measured by unemployment or by wages. In particular, state-by-state changes in unemployment rates between 1996 and 2000 are not significant determinants of state-by-state changes in recipiency rates in any of our analytical specifications.[5] Unemployment levels as of 1996 do help

---

[4]See U.S. Department of Health and Human Services (2000), Table 3.3.A.

[5]In fact, the sign of the coefficient on the change in unemployment is sometimes negative and sometimes positive.

explain the level differences in welfare recipiency declines, where states with higher initial rates of unemployment experienced larger level declines in recipiency. This may reflect that welfare caseload increases that were driven largely by the recession were also more likely to leave aid as the economy improved. It may also distinguish states that recovered economically later and therefore experienced greater caseload declines after 1996 rather than in the 1994–1996 period.

As with the pre-TANF era, we also examined the effects of changes in low-skilled wages. Economic theory suggests that higher low-skilled wages indicate an increase in labor demand and also provide an additional incentive for recipients to leave the rolls. Yet, for the 1996–2000 period, higher wages for the bottom 20 percent of workers are linked to higher welfare recipiency rates, not lower. In other words, in all our specifications, the changes in wages by state have estimated effects in the opposite direction from economic theory and from what we saw for the pre-TANF years. However, it is important to note that neither the levels nor the changes in low-skilled wages are ever remotely statistically significant in the post-TANF analyses.

The central lesson we take from these empirical findings is that the standard relationships linking economic conditions and the evolution of welfare caseloads found in the prereform period do not apply after welfare reform. From a formal statistical perspective, one can mostly ignore economic factors altogether in explaining the extent to which welfare caseloads declined across states.

Demographic characteristics are also less important in the postreform era than earlier. Three demographic factors appear to matter in some specifications: the share of the caseload with three or more children, the nonmarital birth rate, and the share with young children (aged 2 or younger). As with the pre-TANF analysis, the finding for the share of the caseload with three or more children is counterintuitive: States with more large families on the caseload had greater level caseload declines. Nonmarital birth rates, on the other hand, have the expected effect in the TANF era, as they did earlier. States with higher rates in the years leading up to welfare reform had lower declines in caseloads, although this factor shows up as significant only in some specifications for percentage changes in recipiency rates, where one additional birth per

1,000 women increased caseloads by just under 1 percent. Unlike the pre-TANF period, the fraction of the caseload with young children (aged 2 or younger) appears as a systematic determinant of caseload trends in the post-TANF period. A higher value of this fraction tends to increase the growth in caseloads, meaning that a larger share of young families mitigates the extent to which caseloads declined in the post-TANF period. This may result in part from the barriers that parents of very young children face in joining the labor force, but it also reflects the policy choice enacted by the majority of states to exempt parents of young children, typically under age 1, from required work activities. Finally, the noncitizen share of the caseload does not appear to be a significant determinant of state variations, although it is interesting that this factor enters with the opposite sign from that in the prereform period.

Explaining California's Recipiency Rate Decline

Between August 1996 and June 2000, California's recipiency rate fell by 43 percent, below the national average of 51 percent. How would circumstances differ if California had experienced different economic or demographic trends or chosen different TANF policies? In this section, we repeat the exercise conducted in the last chapter, comparing California to the "average" state.[6] Previously, we compared California to Illinois, because of the dramatic differences between the largest states and the rest of the United States. In the TANF era, however, these demographic conditions appear much less important.

Figure 6.2 starts on the left-hand side with California's actual recipiency rate decline, indicated on the first bar. The remaining bars show how much greater (or smaller) the state's recipiency rate change might have been under alternative scenarios. First, consider what would have happened if California's economy had experienced the unemployment and low-skilled wage dynamics as the average. As the second bar shows, this alternative would have had little effect on our recipiency rates, consistent with the low correlation between economic

---

[6]The results in this section are drawn from the specification in column 7 of Appendix Table B.5.A, including all variables whether or not coefficients were significant.

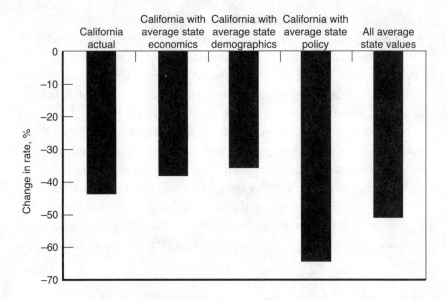

Figure 6.2—Estimated Recipiency Rate Decline in California Under
Alternative Assumptions

characteristics and postreform caseload declines. To the degree there is
an effect from these economic factors, it is to reduce rather than increase
the recipiency rate decline. What if, instead, California had had the same
demographic characteristics of the average state? Our analysis suggests
that, under these alternative circumstances, California would have
actually experienced a smaller caseload decline than actually occurred.

Thus, both economic and demographic circumstances contributed to
increasing the decline in California's welfare caseload over what would
have occurred had it experienced the average situation of other states.
This stands in sharp contrast to the role of these forces in the prereform
years when they led to California's having one of the highest caseload
increases. As noted above, the fact that California's poorer economy
apparently assisted its caseload decline may reflect its later economic
recovery relative to that of the average state, leading to more of
California's recovery occurring during the initial years of welfare reform.
California's demographic conditions, especially the size of its noncitizen
caseload, also contributed to a greater caseload decline. This suggests

that much of the IRCA-induced run-up in state caseloads was temporary.[7]

As we saw in Table 6.2, alternative policy choices would have significantly increased California's caseload reduction. Had California chosen the same policies as the average state, its caseload decline would have been greater than 60 percent. These policies alone explain the gap between California's performance and the national average, since combining all the average state characteristics leads to the national average of 51 percent—a decline that falls between California's actual and its potential under alternative policies.

Economic Factors Affect the National Trend Overall

Our analysis examines the differences across states in the postreform era. Yet many of the most dramatic changes in welfare caseloads appear to be common to all states. These dramatic changes surface as one common effect—a large and negative "intercept"—in our regression analysis. This national trend toward substantially lower caseloads is thus separated out of our regression results, which focus on the effects of the smaller, state-to-state differences in the economy, demographics, and, of course, welfare policy. In particular, the booming economy of the late 1990s surely reduced caseloads in all states. This point holds true regardless of our finding that differences in economic performance across states do little to explain difference in state caseload declines.[8]

The national trend toward lower caseloads may also be driven in part by common effects of welfare reform. For instance, virtually every state adopted a work-first approach to employment services, despite the variation in the time frames for mandatory engagement in work activities. All states may also be "benefiting" from an increased stigma associated with welfare receipt. Of course, we cannot distinguish among the factors that may be causing the large common downward trend in

---

[7]An alternative explanation might be that cases associated with IRCA immigrants were disproportionately two-parent cases, and the two-parent caseload declined much more rapidly than the balance of the caseload in the second half of the 1990s.

[8]It may be the case that economic conditions did not differ significantly enough for our regression analysis to detect the effect of state-level economic conditions.

caseloads. However, our empirical results clearly imply that variation in state TANF policies is the key factor driving *variation* in state welfare caseload declines. For states such as California that have adopted benign TANF policies, the factors driving the national trend toward lower caseloads account for most of the state-specific caseload decline. Thus, our findings are consistent with the argument that common welfare reform effects or the improved economic conditions nationally largely explain California's welfare caseload decline, with more rigorous state-level policies accounting for larger declines elsewhere in the country.

Comparison with Earlier Findings

Because welfare reform is young, relatively few studies have looked specifically at the postreform performance of states. Studies of caseload declines before welfare reform were clearly done to inform our understanding of TANF results, but as long as the economy remains strong, it is difficult to isolate the role of the economy and reform in the national trend. However, we can link our results to two studies that examined the 1996–1998 period. First, the 1999 update by the CEA extended its 1997 time-series analysis to include data through 1998. It concluded that 8 percent of the 1996–1998 decline can be attributed to low unemployment rates and another 10 percent to increases in the minimum wage. The CEA estimates the effects of waivers and TANF policies together; in other words, its estimation procedure does not distinguish between policies put in place as waivers and policies put in place under TANF. The CEA finding on earnings disregards fits with our finding on high benefits, concluding that this policy increases recipiency. Like us, CEA finds that strong sanctions reduce participation. On the other side of the political aisle, Rector and Youssef (1999), writing for the Heritage Foundation, examine percentage caseload reductions between January 1997 and June 1998, using a cross-section regression strategy similar to ours. They conclude that stringent sanctions and immediate work requirements are associated with large percentage drops in caseloads. The first conclusion accords with our results, although we did not find the same effects of work requirements. As with our results, they do not find a significant effect of unemployment rates.

Summary

California's recipiency rate has fallen more slowly than average in the TANF era. Economic and demographic factors outside the control of state program designers do not explain California's relatively small percentage caseload decline under TANF. In the 1996–2000 period, policy choices appear to be the main determinants of state variation in recipiency rate declines. More severe sanction strategies, especially full-family sanctions at the first instance of noncompliance, are associated with significant caseload reductions. Less generous benefits, taking into account both the maximum grant and the income cutoff, are also linked with larger recipiency rate reductions. California is among the most generous states on both of these criteria. Had California chosen policies more like the national average, it would have experienced recipiency rate declines over 60 percent, instead of around 40 percent. For example, Illinois, a moderate sanction, moderate benefit state, experienced an extra 18 percent decline in recipiency, controlling for demographics and economic factors. The economy and other factors that are common across states explain the nationwide trend toward significantly lower recipiency but do not explain state-level differences.

7. Conclusions

In the early 1990s, welfare recipiency rates in California increased relative to those in other states; since welfare reform, the drop in its caseload has lagged behind most states. What explains California's poor performance in reducing its welfare caseload? Our empirical analysis indicates that the principal factors contributing to these trends differ before and after welfare reform. Before the passage of PRWORA, a state's economy and demographic characteristics played consequential roles in its caseload dynamics. With the advent of TANF, the features of a state's welfare program became the most critical factors influencing the decline of its caseload relative to that of other states.

In the 1989–1996 period, California's caseload climbed as much as 50 percent, more than twice the national average. A portion of this greater growth reflects the deeper and longer recession experienced by California compared to other areas of the country. During this recession, workers at the low end of the wage distribution were particularly disadvantaged. These workers saw their real hourly wages drop 90 cents between 1989 and 1996—a period that saw wages for similar workers in the average state decline by only 13 cents. In addition to these poor economic conditions, California also had a relatively large population at above-average risk of welfare recipiency: a significant segment of unmarried women who gave birth and a sizable number of poor immigrants legalized under the 1986 Immigration Reform and Control Act. We found demographic factors (particularly IRCA) and the economic downturn to have played important roles in driving up California's recipiency rate.

Economics and demographics—measured by unemployment rates, low-skilled wage levels, nonmarital birth rates, and immigration—explain most of the state variation in changes in recipiency rates in the preform period, and the combined effect of these variables accounts for the gap between California and other states. According to our estimates for the pre-TANF period, if California's values for the changes in economic and demographic variables were replaced by values experienced by the average state, California's recipiency rate would have *decreased* by 5 percent from 1989 to 1996. This decrease stands in sharp contrast to the 44 percent rise that actually occurred over this seven-year period.

Only a small part of this predicted decrease would have been the result of policy changes. The only policy contributing to the decrease is California's substantial cut in grant levels over this period—about $220 per month in real terms. However, these grant reductions are unlikely to have occurred in a better economy. In addition, the relationship between grant reductions and caseload declines is inconsistent across the time period. In general, welfare waivers appear to explain little of the state variation in welfare recipiency before welfare reform.

In fact, our evidence clearly indicates that California's extraordinarily large IRCA population and the severity of its mid-1990 recession contribute markedly to the growth in its caseloads during the pre-TANF years. Consider California in contrast to another state with a large population and large share of immigrants. Our estimates suggest that California's welfare recipiency would have increased by only 45 percent of its actual value had California had the same small IRCA population as Illinois. California's dismal economic circumstances account for an even more substantial portion of its higher-than-average caseload growth. We estimate that had California faced the same economic conditions as Illinois, its caseload increase would have been cut by two-thirds.

Over the 1996–2000 period, California's caseload dropped by 43 percent, falling short of the 50 percent median for all states. Economic conditions and demographic factors play virtually no role in explaining why California lagged behind other states in lowering its caseload in the postreform period—in fact, California had relative favorable conditions in these dimensions. This is not to say that California's strong economic upturn in the mid-1990s contributed little to reducing its caseloads, nor does it necessarily imply that economic forces had different effects before and after welfare reform. Instead, our empirical findings indicate that differences in state welfare policies far dominate differentials in state economic and demographic characteristics when comparing the performances of states in decreasing their welfare caseloads; policy choices account for two to three times the variation in state caseload trends than is attributable to economic and demographic factors.

California's relatively generous TANF policies go most of the way toward accounting for its low ranking. PRWORA gave states considerable flexibility over their program design, and states adopting more severe sanctions and less generous benefits experienced greater declines in their caseloads in the postreform era. In the design of its TANF program, California selected a higher benefit, lower sanction program than other states. In particular, California established a 50 percent earned income disregard which, combined with a relatively high maximum grant level, creates the highest earned income cutoff in the country. By precluding full-family sanctions, the state also has one of the mildest sanction policies, especially compared to other states that remove an entire family from the grant the first time a recipient does not comply with program requirements.

Overall, our findings reveal a significant association between policy choices and welfare recipiency rates. When we compare California's combination of high benefits and low sanctions to those in other states, we discover that almost all other combinations reduce predicted welfare recipiency rates more than California's. In particular, our results suggest that if California had adopted the opposite strategy of high sanctions and low benefits, its recipiency rates would have dropped an extra 36 percentage points. Thus, California's comparatively weak performance in reducing welfare recipiency in the postreform era is primarily the result of its policy choices.

If recipiency rates were the ultimate measure of welfare reform's success, this conclusion would suggest that California should change its policies. However, recipiency rates should not be the final yardstick of success in welfare reform. Low benefit levels and stringent sanctions certainly reduce caseloads, but this reduction may well come at the cost of substantially lower income for families and reduced well-being for the children of former welfare recipients. Researchers are just beginning to collect data that can address the question of the well-being of families who leave welfare, and we are much further from knowing how these outcomes relate to state policies. Moreover, in their selection of policies, the designers of California's new welfare program not only intended to encourage welfare recipients to work but also to support current participants while working. The state's high benefit strategy certainly achieves this goal—California leads almost all states in the percentage of aided adults involved in unsubsidized employment. In the final accounting, if we want to understand California's successes and shortcomings relative to other states, we need to learn a great deal more about outcomes on many more fronts.

Appendix A

Variable Definitions

1. **Caseload measures:** We constructed monthly state AFDC/TANF recipiency rates using caseload data from DHHS and population data from the U.S. Census Bureau. Recipiency rates are defined to be the total AFDC/TANF caseload per 1,000 women aged 15 to 44. We used both the level and percentage change ((current − base)/base) in the recipiency rate in our regression analysis.
2. **Wage rates:** We used the annual estimate of 20th percentile of state wage distribution from Economic Policy Institute calculations using Current Population Survey data. We used differenced one- and two-year averages of real wage rates in the regression analysis.
3. **Unemployment:** We used monthly unemployment rates (not seasonally adjusted) obtained from the Bureau of Labor Statistics. We used differenced 12- and 24-month averages of unemployment rates in the regression analysis.
4. **Nonmarital birth rates:** Nonmarital birth counts were constructed from annual public use natality files prepared by the National Center for Health Statistics. The rates were normalized per 1,000 women aged 15 to 44 and averaged over a five-year period including the base month (e.g., 1985–1989 in the pre-TANF regressions). We made adjustments for California and Texas to reflect changes in methods for determining mother's marital status.
5. **IRCA immigration rates:** Data on IRCA immigration counts by state of intended residence were obtained from the Immigration and Naturalization Service. Counts were normalized per 1,000 women aged 15 to 44.
6. **AFDC/TANF caseload demographic measures:** Measures of the share of cases with children under age 2, cases with three or more children, noncitizens, adults who have 0–9 years of schooling, and adults by race/ethnicity are drawn from case characteristics data

reported to the DHHS. Data before FFY 1997 were obtained from DHHS's annual AFDC characteristics reports. Data for FFY 1999 were obtained from DHHS (2000).

7. **Pre-TANF policy measures:** Data on maximum benefit levels (three-person assistance unit) and state waiver activity were obtained from DHHS. Benefit levels were normalized to March 1999 dollars, and we used differences in real benefit levels in the regression analysis.

8. **TANF policy measures:** Data on state TANF policies were obtained from the Administration for Children & Families, U.S. DHHS. We identified "high," "moderate," and "low" sanction states according to the following classification scheme: high sanction states implement full-family sanctions after a single episode of noncooperation with work program requirements; moderate sanction states implement full-family sanctions only after multiple episodes of noncooperation; and low sanction states implement maximum partial-grant sanctions. We partitioned states into high, moderate, and low benefit categories based on maximum benefit levels and earned income cutoffs. Low benefit states were defined to have earned income cutoffs below $558 per month for a family of three after six months with earnings.[1] We defined high benefit states to have earned income cutoffs above $1,000 per month for a three-person assistance unit after six months with earnings, and a corresponding maximum benefit level above $400. States that do not fall into the high or low benefit categories were classified as moderate benefit states.

---

[1] This cutoff level is equivalent to 25 hours per week of employment at $5.15 per hour. The one-parent work participation requirement in effect in March 1999 was 25 hours per week, and the federal minimum wage at that time was $5.15 per hour. Thus, low benefit states are those in which full adult participation in employment at the minimum wage will move an assistance unit with one adult and two children off aid.

Table A.1

Waiver Provisions Granted Before August 1996, by State

State	Full-Family Sanction	Termination Time Limit	Work Requirements Time Limit	Earnings Disregard	JOBS Exemption	Family Cap
Alabama	—	—	—	—	—	—
Alaska	—	—	—	—	—	—
Arizona	—	—	—	—	—	Y
Arkansas	—	—	—	—	—	Y
California	—	—	Y	Y	—	—
Colorado	—	—	Y	Y	—	—
Connecticut	Y	Y	—	Y	Y	Y
Delaware	Y	Y	Y	Y	Y	Y
District of Columbia	—	—	—	—	—	—
Florida	—	Y	—	Y	—	—
Georgia	—	—	—	—	—	Y
Hawaii	—	—	—	—	—	—
Idaho	—	—	—	—	—	—
Illinois	Y	Y	Y	Y	—	Y
Indiana	—	—	—	Y	Y	Y
Iowa	Y	Y	—	Y	Y	—
Kansas	—	—	—	—	—	—
Kentucky	—	—	—	—	—	—
Louisiana	—	—	—	—	—	—
Maine	—	—	—	—	—	—
Maryland	—	—	—	—	—	Y
Massachusetts	Y	—	Y	Y	Y	Y
Michigan	Y	—	Y	Y	Y	—
Minnesota	—	—	—	Y	—	—
Mississippi	Y	—	—	Y	—	Y
Missouri	—	—	Y	Y	—	—
Montana	—	—	Y	Y	Y	—
Nebraska	Y	Y	—	—	Y	—
Nevada	—	—	—	—	—	—
New Hampshire	—	—	—	—	—	—
New Jersey	—	—	—	—	Y	Y
New Mexico	—	—	—	—	—	—
New York	—	—	—	—	—	—
North Carolina	—	—	—	—	—	—
North Dakota	—	—	—	—	—	—
Ohio	—	—	—	—	—	—
Oklahoma	—	—	—	—	—	—
Oregon	Y	—	—	—	Y	—
Pennsylvania	—	—	—	—	—	—
Rhode Island	—	—	—	—	—	—
South Carolina	—	—	—	—	—	—
South Dakota	Y	—	Y	—	—	—
Tennessee	—	—	—	—	—	—
Texas	—	—	—	—	—	—
Utah	Y	—	—	Y	Y	—
Vermont	—	—	Y	Y	Y	—
Virginia	Y	Y	Y	Y	Y	Y
Washington	—	—	—	—	—	—
West Virginia	Y	—	—	—	—	—
Wisconsin	Y	Y	—	Y	Y	Y
Wyoming	—	—	—	—	—	—

Table A.2

TANF Program Characteristics, by State

State	Full-Family Sanction		Benefits			Immediate Work Requirement	Time Limits = 60 mo
	Immediate	Eventual	Low	Moderate	High		
Alabama	—	Y	Y	—	—	Y	Y
Alaska	—	—	—	—	Y	—	Y
Arizona	—	Y	Y	—	—	—	Y
Arkansas	—	Y	—	Y	—	Y	Less
California	—	—	—	—	Y	—	—
Colorado	—	Y	Y	—	—	—	Y
Connecticut	—	Y	—	—	Y	Y	Less
Delaware	—	Y	Y	—	—	—	Less
District of Columbia	—	—	—	Y	—	—	Y
Florida	Y	Y	—	Y	—	Y	Less
Georgia	—	Y	Y	—	—	Y	Less
Hawaii	—	—	—	—	Y	—	Y
Idaho	Y	Y	Y	—	—	Y	Less
Illinois	—	Y	—	Y	—	—	—
Indiana	—	—	—	Y	—	—	Y
Iowa	—	Y	—	Y	—	Y	Y
Kansas	Y	Y	—	Y	—	Y	Y
Kentucky	—	—	Y	—	—	—	Y
Louisiana	—	Y	Y	—	—	—	Y
Maine	—	—	—	—	Y	—	Y
Maryland	Y	Y	Y	—	—	Y	Y
Massachusetts	—	Y	—	—	Y	Y	—
Michigan	Y	Y	—	Y	—	Y	—
Minnesota	—	—	—	Y	—	—	Y
Mississippi	Y	Y	Y	—	—	—	Y
Missouri	—	—	Y	—	—	—	Y
Montana	—	—	—	Y	—	—	Y
Nebraska	Y	Y	—	Y	—	Y	Y
Nevada	—	Y	—	Y	—	—	Y
New Hampshire	—	—	—	—	Y	Y	Y
New Jersey	—	Y	—	Y	—	—	Y
New Mexico	—	Y	—	Y	—	Y	Y
New York	—	—	—	—	Y	—	Y
North Carolina	—	Y	Y	—	—	—	Y
North Dakota	—	Y	—	Y	—	—	Y
Ohio	Y	Y	—	Y	—	—	Less
Oklahoma	Y	Y	—	Y	—	Y	Y
Oregon	—	Y	—	—	Y	Y	Y
Pennsylvania	—	Y	—	Y	—	—	Y
Rhode Island	—	—	—	—	Y	—	—
South Carolina	Y	Y	Y	—	—	—	Y
South Dakota	—	Y	—	Y	—	Y	Y
Tennessee	Y	Y	Y	—	—	Y	Y
Texas	—	—	Y	—	—	Y	—
Utah	—	Y	—	—	Y	Y	Less
Vermont	—	Y	—	—	Y	—	Y
Virginia	Y	Y	—	Y	—	Y	Y
Washington	—	—	—	—	Y	Y	Y
West Virginia	—	Y	Y	—	—	—	Y
Wisconsin	Y	Y	—	—	Y	Y	Y
Wyoming	Y	Y	Y	—	—	Y	Y

Appendix B

Regression Results

This appendix provides detailed ordinary least squares regression results for the analyses described in Chapters 4 to 6. Our estimation conducts a simple cross-section analysis using data on changes (i.e., on first differences) experienced by the 50 states plus the District of Columbia (51 observations). The regressors are described in Chapter 3 with additional information provided in Appendix A. The dependent variable in each regression is the change in welfare recipiency rates between the beginning date and end date of the analysis period. Each regression is conducted using the change measured in levels or percentage terms, with separate tables for each:

A—Percentage change in recipiency rates
B—Level change in recipiency rates

The regression results are then presented in five sets of tables:

Determinants of state variation in the pre-TANF period:

Tables B.1.A and B.1.B, July 1989 to August 1996
Tables B.2.A and B.2.B, July 1989 to August 1992
Tables B.3.A and B.3.B, August 1992 to August 1996

Determinants of state variation in the post-TANF period:

Tables B.4.A and B.4.B, August 1996 to June 2000
Tables B.5.A and B.5.B, August 1996 to June 2000, interacted

Each table presents four to nine different specifications. The preferred specifications discussed in Chapters 5 and 6 are indicated with an asterisk.

The treatment of lagged economic variables creates an important distinction between our cross-section approach and time-series models with complex lag structures that are commonly used to describe the

Table B.1.A

Determinants of State Variation in the Pre-TANF Period: Dependent Variable— Percentage Change in Welfare Recipiency Rate, July 1989 to August 1996
(t-statistics in parentheses)

Independent Variables	Specification					
	1	2	3	4	5	6
Economic Factors						
Δ Unemployment rate (av. 8/88–7/89) – av. (9/95–8/96))	0.077 (2.64)	0.104 (4.75)		0.100 (3.69)	0.093 (3.60)	0.099 (4.75)
Δ 20th percentile wage (1989–1996)	–0.093 (–1.09)	–0.210 (–2.88)		–0.177 (–2.24)	–0.162 (–2.13)	–0.159 (–2.30)
Demographic Factors						
Nonmarital birth rate (av. 1985–1989))	0.009 (1.02)		0.016 (1.40)	0.0004 (0.05)	0.002 (0.27)	–0.004 (–0.74)
IRCA legalization rate	0.001 (0.80)		0.0006 (0.41)	0.001 (1.07)	0.001 (1.18)	0.002 (2.50)
% with 3 or more children (FFY 1989)	–0.020 (–1.73)		–0.040 (–3.24)	–0.014 (–1.33)	–0.013 (–1.29)	–0.014 (–1.88)
% with child aged 0–2 (FFY 1989)	0.0003 (0.03)		0.008 (0.91)	0.003 (0.43)	0.003 (0.52)	
% black case head (FFY 1989)	–0.0003 (0.16)		–0.001 (–0.53)	–0.001 (–0.55)	–0.002 (–0.83)	
% Hispanic case head (FFY 1989)	0.004 (1.12)		0.006 (1.56)	0.001 (0.34)	0.0009 (0.33)	
% Asian case head (FFY 1989)	0.003 (0.81)		0.009 (2.23)	–0.002 (–0.44)	–0.001 (–0.33)	
% Native American case head (FFY 1989)	0.002 (0.45)		–0.002 (–0.39)	–0.002 (–0.55)	–0.002 (–0.64)	
Policy Factors						
Δ Maximum aid payment (7/1989–7/1996)		0.002 (3.03)	0.0004 (0.39)	0.002 (2.99)	0.002 (2.74)	0.002 (3.50)
Waiver: full–family sanction		–0.112 (–1.43)	–0.201 (–1.83)	–0.093 (–1.09)	–0.098 (–1.22)	–0.086 (–1.17)
Waiver: termination time limit		0.148 (1.71)	0.246 (2.00)	0.139 (1.46)	0.168 (1.95)	0.144 (1.88)
Waiver: work requirement time limit		0.031 (0.41)	0.027 (0.25)	0.016 (0.20)		
Waiver: earnings disregard		0.073 (0.92)	–0.024 (–0.22)	0.085 (0.99)		
Waiver: JOBS exemptions		–0.149 (–2.01)	–0.072 (–0.68)	–0.174 (–2.10)	–0.135 (–1.83)	–0.126 (–1.82)
Waiver: family cap		–0.079 (–1.30)	0.022 (0.23)	–0.024 (–0.33)		
Adjusted R-squared	0.5090	0.6483	0.3709	0.645	0.655	0.683

Table B.1.B

Determinants of State Variation in the Pre-TANF Period: Dependent Variable—Change in Level of Welfare Recipiency Rate, July 1989 to August 1996
(t-statistics in parentheses)

Independent Variables	Specification					
	1	2	3	4	5	6
Economic Factors						
Δ Unemployment rate (av. 8/88–7/89) – av. (9/95–8/96))	6.390 (4.39)	8.233 (5.85)		7.102 (4.87)	6.907 (4.85)	7.279 (6.17)
Δ 20th percentile wage (1989–1996)	0.887 (0.21)	–8.141 (–1.73)		–2.553 (–0.60)	–0.882 (–0.21)	–2.578 (–0.66)
Demographic Factors						
Nonmarital birth rate (av. (1985–1989))	1.207 (2.68)		1.770 (2.85)	0.864 (1.77)	1.016 (2.16)	0.615 (2.16)
IRCA legalization rate	0.101 (1.82)		0.051 (0.66)	0.0087 (1.51)	0.096 (1.69)	0.142 (3.20)
% with 3 or more children (FFY 1989)	–1.978 (–3.32)		–2.977 (–4.36)	–1.678 (–2.93)	–1.687 (–2.98)	–1.585 (–3.81)
% with child aged 0–2 (FFY 1989)	–.0348 (–0.93)		0.023 (0.05)	–0.342 (–0.95)	–0.229 (–0.65)	
% black case head (FFY 1989)	–0.0175 (–0.17)		–0.048 (–0.31)	–0.012 (–0.11)	–0.071 (–0.70)	
% Hispanic case head (FFY 1989)	0.223 (1.40)		0.433 (2.08)	0.191 (1.18)	0.141 (0.90)	
% Asian case head (FFY 1989)	0.211 (1.09)		0.617 (2.86)	0.055 (0.29)	0.062 (0.33)	
% Native American case head (FFY 1989)	0.190 (1.06)		0.027 (0.11)	0.096 (0.51)	0.070 (0.40)	
Policy Factors						
Δ Maximum aid payment (7/1989–7/1996)		0.192 (2.28)	–0.027 (–0.53)	0.068 (1.60)	0.052 (1.31)	0.086 (2.52)
Waiver: full-family sanction		–5.757 (–1.14)	–10.093 (–1.68)	–3.832 (–0.83)	–4.814 (–1.09)	–4.163 (–1.00)
Waiver: termination time limit		6.827 (1.22)	13.212 (1.97)	6.586 (1.28)	7.444 (1.57)	5.265 (1.21)
Waiver: work requirement time limit		3.946 (0.83)	3.382 (0.57)	1.838 (0.41)		
Waiver: earnings disregard		2.963 (0.58)	–3.027 (–0.50)	3.435 (0.74)		
Waiver: JOBS exemptions		–9.632 (–2.01)	–0.654 (–0.11)	–7.217 (–1.61)	–6.324 (–1.55)	–5.754 (–1.46)
Waiver: family cap		–5.870 (–1.50)	–3.901 (–0.75)	–5.377 (–1.36)		
Adjusted R-squared	0.7145	0.6543	0.5558	0.756	0.754	0.760

Table B.2.A

Determinants of State Variation in the Pre-TANF Period: Dependent Variable— Percentage Change in Welfare Recipiency Rate, July 1989 to August 1992
(t–statistics in parentheses)

Independent Variables	Specification			
	1	2	3	4
Economic Factors				
Δ Unemployment rate (av. (8/88 – 7/89) – av. (9/95 – 8/92))	0.032	0.035	0.042	0.048
	(1.31)	(1.36)	(1.76)	(2.62)
Δ 20th percentile wage (1989–1992)	–0.234	–0.237	–0.207	–0.154
	(–1.76)	(–1.68)	(–1.58)	(–1.76)
Demographic Factors				
Nonmarital birth rate (av. (1985–1989))	–0.005	0.001	–0.0009	–0.005
	(–0.47)	(0.10)	(–0.09)	(–0.94)
IRCA legalization rate	0.001	0.0004	0.0003	0.001
	(0.84)	(0.3.0)	(0.29)	(1.32)
% with 3 or more children (FFY 1989)	–0.016	–0.009	–0.008	–0.007
	(–1.42)	(–0.77)	(–0.73)	(–0.88)
% with child aged 0–2 (FFY 1989)	0.006	0.009	0.007	
	(0.70)	(1.10)	(0.88)	
% black case head (FFY 1989)	0.0008	–0.002	–0.0009	
	(0.39)	(–0.70)	(–0.46)	
% Hispanic case head (FFY 1989)	0.003	0.0004	0.001	
	(0.79)	(0.13)	(0.36)	
% Asian case head (FFY 1989)	0.0005	–0.001	–0.001	
	(0.13)	(–0.25)	(–0.29)	
% Native American case head (FFY 1989)	–0.0007	–0.001	–0.0008	
	(–0.18)	(–0.34)	(–0.23)	
Policy Factors				
Δ Maximum aid payment (7/1989–7/1992)	0.002	0.002	0.002	0.002
	(1.72)	(1.25)	(1.37)	(2.12)
Waiver: full–family sanction		–0.185	–0.179	–0.169
		(–1.99)	(–2.04)	(–2.14)
Waiver: termination time limit		0.208	0.211	0.193
		(1.97)	(2.21)	(2.29)
Waiver: work requirement time limit		–0.023		
		(–0.25)		
Waiver: earnings disregard		–0.003		
		(–0.03)		
Waiver: JOBS exemptions		–0.071	–0.063	–0.056
		(–0.79)	(–0.79)	(–0.75)
Waiver: family cap		0.071		
		(0.82)		
Adjusted R-squared	0.239	0.287	0.330	0.384

Table B.2.B
Determinants of State Variation in the Pre-TANF Period: Dependent Variable—
Change in Level of Welfare Recipiency Rate, July 1989 to August 1992
(t–statistics in parentheses)

Independent Variables	Specification 1	2	3	4
Economic Factors				
Δ Unemployment rate (av. 8/88 –	1.626	2.164	2.026	2.361
7/89) – av. (9/91–8/92))	(1.80)	(2.23)	(2.30)	(3.38)
Δ 20th percentile wage	–4.297	–2.224	–3.013	–2.711
(1989–1992)	(–0.87)	(–0.42)	(–0.62)	(–0.68)
Demographic Factors				
Nonmarital birth rate	0.272	0.318	0.380	0.264
(av. (1985–1989))	(0.75)	(0.80)	(1.05)	(1.27)
IRCA legalization rate	0.070	0.047	0.046	0.084
	(1.58)	(1.04)	(1.06)	(2.67)
% with 3 or more children	–1.462	–1.183	–1.168	–0.931
(FFY 1989)	(–3.46)	(–2.63)	(–2.78)	(–2.99)
% with child aged 0–2	–0.189	–0.193	–0.154	
(FFY 1989)	(–0.65)	(–0.63)	(–0.56)	
% with black case head	0.052	0.015	–0.007	
(FFY 1989)	(0.69)	(0.16)	(–0.09)	
% Hispanic case head	0.230	0.196	0.179	
(FFY 1989)	(1.93)	(1.56)	(1.54)	
% Asian case head	0.128	0.069	0.065	
(FFY 1989)	(0.88)	(0.46)	(0.46)	
% Native American case head	0.066	0.092	0.061	
(FFY 1989)	(0.47)	(0.58)	(0.45)	
Policy Factors				
Δ Maximum aid payment	0.045	0.025	0.025	0.065
(7/1989–7/1992)	(0.88)	(0.48)	(0.52)	(1.82)
Waiver: full–family		–6.129	–6.425	–7.098
sanction		(–1.76)	(–1.98)	(–2.36)
Waiver: termination		6.760	7.202	6.554
time limit		(1.71)	(2.03)	(2.05)
Waiver: work requirement		–0.792		
time limit		(–0.23)		
Waiver: earnings		1.195		
disregard		(0.34)		
Waiver: JOBS		–2.650	–2.574	–1.688
exemptions		(–0.79)	(–0.87)	(–0.59)
Waiver: family cap		–1.310		
		(–0.41)		
Adjusted R-squared	0.482	0.504	0.542	0.555

Table B.3.A

Determinants of State Variation in the Pre-TANF Period: Dependent Variable—Percentage Change in Welfare Recipiency Rate, August 1992 to August 1996
(t-statistics in parentheses)

Independent Variables	Specification			
	1	2	3	4
Economic Factors				
Δ Unemployment rate (av. 9/91 –	0.025	0.018	0.022	0.031
8/92) – av. (9/95–8/96))	(1.59)	(1.00)	(1.32)	(2.14)
Δ 20th percentile wage	−0.094	−0.010	−0.077	−0.170
(1992–1996)	(−1.46)	(−1.27)	(−1.16)	(−3.13)
Demographic Factors				
Nonmarital birth rate	0.012	0.013	0.013	0.003
(av. (1988–1992))	(2.57)	(2.43)	(2.63)	(0.84)
IRCA legalization rate	0.0003	−0.0001	0.00006	0.0006
	(0.45)	(−0.17)	(0.09)	(1.18)
% with 3 or more children	−0.011	−0.010	−0.012	−0.006
(FFY 1992)	(−1.85)	(−1.63)	(−1.96)	(−1.21)
% with child aged 0–2	−0.010	−0.010	−0.010	
(FFY 1992)	(−1.77)	(−1.71)	(−1.59)	
% black case head	−0.0007	−0.0008	−0.001	
(FFY 1992)	(−0.68)	(−0.67)	(−0.93)	
% Hispanic case head	0.001	0.002	0.001	
(FFY 1992)	(0.59)	(0.81)	(0.70)	
% Asian case head	0.004	0.004	0.005	
(FFY 1992)	(1.86)	(1.70)	(1.93)	
% Native American case head	−0.002	−0.003	−0.002	
(FFY 1992)	(−1.14)	(−1.35)	(−1.19)	
Policy Factors				
Δ Maximum aid payment	−0.0003	−0.0002	−0.0004	−0.000001
(7/1992–7/1996)	(−0.39)	(−0.30)	(−0.58)	(−0.00)
Waiver: full-family		−0.022	−0.015	0.002
sanction		(−0.42)	(−0.30)	(0.03)
Waiver: termination		0.088	0.066	0.0127
time limit		(1.44)	(1.19)	(0.23)
Waiver: work requirement		0.070		
time limit		(1.36)		
Waiver: earnings		−0.035		
disregard		(−0.62)		
Waiver: JOBS		−0.031	−0.046	−0.055
exemptions		(−0.60)	(−0.97)	(−1.15)
Waiver: family cap		−0.052		
		(−1.11)		
Adjusted R-squared	0.506	0.505	0.496	0.418

Table B.3.B

Determinants of State Variation in the Pre-TANF Period: Dependent Variable— Change in Level of Welfare Recipiency Rate, August 1992 to August 1996
(t-statistics in parentheses)

Independent Variables	Specification			
	1	2	3	4
Economic Factors				
Δ Unemployment rate (av. (9/91–	3.393	2.975	3.224	3.543
8/92) – av. (9/95–8/96))	(2.63)	(1.97)	(2.27)	(2.98)
Δ 20th percentile wage	−7.244	−9.810	−6.344	−12.160
(1988–1992)	(−1.35)	(−1.47)	(−1.13)	(−2.77)
Demographic Factors				
Nonmarital birth rate	1.153	1.115	1.230	0.449
(av. (1985–1989))	(2.90)	(2.40)	(2.85)	(1.48)
IRCA legalization rate	0.013	−0.007	0.003	0.062
	(0.23)	(−0.12)	(0.05)	(1.42)
% with 3 or more children	−1.156	−1.105	−1.210	−0.833
(FFY 1992)	(−2.39)	(−2.11)	(−2.35)	(−2.00)
% with child aged 0–2	−0.351	−0.360	−0.355	
(FFY 1992)	(−0.74)	(−0.70)	(−0.70)	
% black case head	−0.089	−0.065	−0.106	
(FFY 1992)	(−1.00)	(−0.62)	(−1.13)	
% Hispanic case head	0.088	0.127	0.095	
(FFY 1992)	(0.59)	(0.78)	(0.60)	
% Asian case head	0.209	0.189	0.228	
(FFY 1992)	(1.06)	(0.86)	(1.11)	
% Native American case head	−0.156	−0.169	−0.160	
(FFY 1992)	(−1.05)	(−1.02)	(−1.03)	
Policy Factors				
Δ Maximum aid payment	−0.026	−0.005	−0.032	0.013
(7/1992–7/1996)	(−0.45)	(−0.08)	(−0.51)	(0.21)
Waiver: full-family		−0.641	−0.821	0.532
sanction		(−0.15)	(−0.19)	(0.13)
Waiver: termination		4.432	3.733	−0.217
time limit		(0.85)	(0.79)	(−0.05)
Waiver: work requirement		3.639		
time limit		(0.84)		
Waiver: earnings		−0.460		
disregard		(−0.09)		
Waiver: JOBS		−0.947	−1.743	−1.642
exemptions		(−0.21)	(−0.44)	(−0.43)
Waiver: family cap		−5.879		
		(−1.48)		
Adjusted R-squared	0.505	0.481	0.475	0.448

Table B.4.A

Determinants of State Variation in the Postreform Period: Dependent Variable—Percentage Change in Welfare Recipiency Rate, August 1996 to June 2000

(t-statistics in parentheses)

Independent Variables	Specification								
	1	2	3	4	5	6	7	8	9
Economic Factors									
ΔUnemployment rate (av. (9/95–8/96) – av. (4/98–6/00))	-0.078 (-1.71)	-0.022 (0.81)		-0.011 (-0.28)	-0.021 (-0.54)	-0.010 (-0.25)	-0.019 (-0.42)	-0.042 (-1.29)	-0.050 (-1.65)
Δ20th percentile wage (1996–2000)	0.168 (1.63)	0.162 (2.16)		0.145 (1.73)			0.105 (1.07)		
Unemployment rate (1996)							-0.020 (-0.72)	-0.035 (-1.67)	
20th percentile wage (1996)							0.013 (0.31)		
Demographic Factors									
Nonmarital birth rate (av. (1992–1996))	0.009 (1.66)		0.005 (1.13)	0.006 (1.22)	0.004 (0.93)	0.005 (1.01)	0.009 (1.41)	0.010 (2.24)	
% adults not citizen (FFY 1996)	0.007 (1.51)		-0.006 (-1.27)	-0.004 (-0.90)	-0.006 (-1.19)	-0.008 (-1.38)	-0.004 (-0.73)	-0.004 (-1.41)	
% adults 0–9 years of schooling (FFY 1996)	-0.005 (-1.02)		0.002 (0.40)	0.00002 (0.00)	0.001 (0.34)	0.002 (0.53)	0.001 (0.15)		
% with 3 or more children (FFY 1996)	-0.010 (-1.08)		-0.124 (-1.61)	-0.010 (-1.39)	-0.013 (-1.61)	-0.012 (-1.44)	-0.010 (-1.35)	-0.009 (-1.62)	-0.009 (-1.53)
% with child aged 0–2 (FFY 1996)	0.005 (0.60)		0.010 (1.61)	0.008 (1.20)	0.011 (1.69)	0.011 (1.57)	0.008 (1.09)	0.009 (1.41)	0.011 (1.95)

Table B.4.A. (continued)

Independent Variables	Specification								
	1	2	3	4	5	6	7	8	9
% black case head	-0.002		0.0008	0.0005	0.0007	0.0008	0.000		
(FFY 1996)	(-1.35)		(0.64)	(0.36)	(0.55)	(0.58)	(0.05)		
% Hispanic case head	-0.004		0.0009	0.0004	0.0005	0.0009	0.000		
(FFY 1996)	(-1.46)		(0.41)	(0.17)	(0.23)	(0.38)	(0.01)		
% Asian case head	0.002		0.002	0.001	0.002	0.002	0.001		
(FFY 1996)	(0.75)		(0.83)	(0.66)	(0.83)	(0.83)	(0.68)		
% Native American case head	0.001		0.0007	0.001	0.001	0.0006	0.001		
(FFY 1996)	(0.53)		(0.33)	(0.47)	(0.44)	(0.25)	(0.28)		
Policy Factors									
High sanction		-0.216	-0.242	-0.225	-0.235	-0.233	-0.224	-0.244	-0.234
		(-4.53)	(-4.39)	(-4.02)	(-4.10)	(-3.66)	(-3.90)	(-5.15)	(-5.00)
Moderate sanction		-0.104	-0.155	-0.130	-0.150	-0.145	-0.131	-0.148	-0.132
		(-2.52)	(-3.10)	(-2.54)	(-2.91)	(-2.74)	(-2.50)	(-3.63)	(-3.20)
Moderate benefits		0.012	-0.033	-0.044	-0.031	-0.038	-0.035	-0.043	0.027
		(0.28)	(-0.60)	(-0.82)	(-0.57)	(-0.66)	(-0.59)	(-0.90)	(0.61)
Low benefits		-0.121	-0.181	-0.180	-0.173	-0.192	-0.156	-0.154	-0.094
		(-2.67)	(-2.85)	(-2.80)	(-2.63)	(2.65)	(-2.16)	(-3.12)	(-2.11)
Immediate time frame for work						0.017			
						(0.40)			
Lifetime time limit < 5 years						-0.086			
						(-1.08)			
Lifetime time limit = 5 years						-0.014			
						(0.20)			
Adjusted R-squared	0.160	0.484	0.466	0.485	0.456	0.438	0.456	0.513	0.473

71

Table B.4.B

Determinants of State Variation in the Postreform Period: Dependent Variable—Change in Level of Welfare Recipiency Rate, August 1996 to June 2000

(t-statistics in parentheses)

	Specification								
	1	2	3	4	5	6	7	8	9
Economic Factors									
ΔUnemployment rate (av. (9/95–8/96) – av. (4/98–6/00))	2.978	6.546		6.963	5.447	6.529	4.070	1.418	5.863
	(0.83)	(2.57)		(2.00)	(1.45)	(1.75)	(1.02)	(0.47)	(1.94)
Δ20th percentile wage (1996–2000)	23.106	20.998		21.262			12.466		
	(2.87)	(3.01)		(2.78)			(1.45)		
Unemployment rate (1996)							−4.621	−6.300	
							(−1.93)	(−3.28)	
20th percentile wage (1996)							0.880		
							(0.25)		
Demographic Factors									
Nonmarital birth rate (av. (1992–1996))	0.144		−0.410	−0.050	−0.234	−0.046	0.524	0.755	
	(0.33)		(−0.92)	(−0.12)	(−0.51)	(−0.10)	(0.99)	(1.92)	
% adults not citizen (FFY 1996)	−0.049		−0.953	−0.807	−1.027	−0.935	−0.673	−0.398	
	(−0.13)		(−1.96)	(−1.80)	(−2.14)	(−1.84)	(−1.55)	(−1.38)	
% adults 0–9 years of schooling (FFY 1996)	−0.644		−0.149	−0.295	−0.089	−0.057	−0.183		
	(−1.81)		(−0.36)	(−0.77)	(−0.22)	(−0.14)	(−0.46)		
% with 3 or more children (FFY 1996)	−1.343		−1.678	−1.369	−1.651	−1.245	−1.313	−0.840	−0.893
	(−1.89)		(−2.19)	(−1.96)	(−2.18)	(−1.58)	(−1.93)	(−1.66)	(−1.57)
% with child aged 0–2 (FFY 1996)	−0.038		0.909	0.129	0.599	0.345	−0.019	0.107	0.380
	(−0.06)		(1.44)	(0.21)	(0.91)	(0.53)	(−0.03)	(0.19)	(0.64)

Table B.4.B (continued)

	Specification								
	1	2	3	4	5	6	7	8	9
% black case head	-0.022		0.131	0.121	0.159	0.135	0.056		
(FFY 1996)	(-0.19)		(1.00)	(1.00)	(1.22)	(1.05)	(0.45)		
% Hispanic case head	0.097		0.276	0.345	0.366	0.320	0.291		
(FFY 1996)	(0.52)		(1.29)	(1.72)	(1.67)	(1.46)	(1.45)		
% Asian case head	0.164		0.196	0.138	0.192	0.168	0.170		
(FFY 1996)	(0.82)		(0.96)	(0.74)	(0.95)	(0.85)	(0.93)		
% Native American case head	0.278		0.316	0.257	0.249	0.122	0.193		
(FFY 1996)	(1.33)		(1.44)	(1.27)	(1.12)	(0.54)	(0.97)		
Policy Factors									
High sanction		-8.963	-11.41	-11.82	-13.27	-16.79	-12.04	-12.96	-7.939
		(-2.02)	(-2.09)	(-2.32)	(-2.40)	(-2.86)	(-2.40)	(-2.97)	(-1.69)
Moderate sanction		-2.31	-9.59	-8.08	-10.97	-11.26	-8.623	-7.704	-4.385
		(-0.60)	(-1.93)	(-1.73)	(-2.20)	(-2.30)	(-1.88)	(-2.05)	(-1.06)
Moderate benefits		1.249	-0.155	-2.483	-0.576	0.903	-1.532	-1.132	2.123
		(0.30)	(-0.03)	(-0.50)	(-0.11)	(0.17)	(-0.30)	(-0.26)	(0.47)
Low benefits		-8.220	-8.760	-11.82	-10.83	-10.07	-8.406	-7.954	-5.218
		(-1.94)	(-1.39)	(-2.02)	(-1.70)	(-1.51)	(-1.33)	(-1.76)	(-1.17)
Immediate time frame for work						8.097			
						(2.00)			
Lifetime time limit < 5 years						-4.013			
						(-0.54)			
Lifetime time limit = 5 years						3.751			
						(0.59)			
Adjusted R-squared	0.161	0.266	0.136	0.297	0.162	0.215	0.319	0.328	0.132

Table B.5.A

Determinants of State Variation in the Postreform Period: Dependent Variable—Percentage Change in Welfare Recipiency Rate, August 1996 to June 2000
(t-statistics in parentheses)

	Specification								
	1	2	3	4	5	6	7	8	9
Economic Factors									
Δ Unemployment rate (av. (9/95–8/96) – av. (4/98–6/00))	-0.078 (-1.71)	-0.018 (-0.63)		-0.011 (-0.26)	-0.023 (-0.57)	-0.018 (-0.36)	-0.039 (-0.94)	-0.042 (-1.23)	-0.024 (-0.74)
Δ 20th percentile wage (1996–2000)	0.168 (1.63)	0.161 (2.04)		0.138 (1.54)		0.099 (0.93)			
Unemployment rate (1996)						-0.020 (-0.67)	-0.035 (-1.43)	-0.036 (-1.63)	
20th percentile wage (1996)						0.013 (0.31)			
Demographic Factors									
Nonmarital birth rate (av. (1992–1996))	0.009 (1.66)		0.004 (0.86)	0.005 (1.01)	0.003 (0.68)	0.008 (1.23)	0.008 (1.38)	0.009 (2.06)	0.005 (1.32)
% adults not citizen (FFY 1996)	0.007 (1.51)		-0.005 (-1.03)	-0.004 (-0.70)	-0.005 (-0.92)	-0.003 (-0.61)	-0.004 (-0.78)	-0.004 (-1.30)	-0.005 (-1.45)
% adults 0–9 years of schooling (FFY 1996)	-0.005 (-1.02)		0.002 (0.46)	0.0002 (0.05)	0.002 (0.38)	0.001 (0.22)	0.002 (0.42)		
% with 3 or more children (FFY 1996)	-0.010 (-1.08)		-0.013 (-1.59)	-0.011 (-1.28)	-0.013 (-1.59)	-0.010 (-1.24)	-0.012 (-1.48)	-0.009 (-1.51)	-0.009 (-1.46)
% with child aged 0–2 (FFY 1996)	0.005 (0.60)		0.014 (1.96)	0.011 (1.40)	0.015 (2.02)	0.011 (1.31)	0.012 (1.57)	0.012 (1.69)	0.014 (2.11)

Table B.5.A (continued)

	Specification								
	1	2	3	4	5	6	7	8	9
% black case head (FFY 1996)	-0.002		0.001	0.0007	0.0009	0.0003	0.0005		
	(-1.35)		(0.79)	(0.50)	(0.68)	(0.21)	(0.32)		
% Hispanic case head (FFY 1996)	-0.004		0.0007	0.0001	0.0003	-0.000	0.0000		
	(-1.46)		(0.31)	(0.06)	(0.12)	(-0.04)	(0.04)		
% Asian case head (FFY 1996)	0.002		0.002	0.001	0.002	0.001	0.002		
	(0.75)		(0.89)	(0.69)	(0.90)	(0.67)	(0.90)		
% Native American case head (FFY 1996)	0.001		0.001	0.001	0.001	0.0009	0.001		
	(0.53)		(0.48)	(0.59)	(0.59)	(0.37)	(0.34)		
Policy Factors									
High sanction, high benefit		-0.315	-0.367	-0.352	-0.346	-0.368	-0.374	-0.387	-0.343
		(-2.43)	(-2.62)	(-2.45)	(-2.35)	(-2.50)	(-2.59)	(-3.05)	(-2.70)
High sanction, moderate benefit		-0.195	-0.276	-0.264	-0.264	-0.264	-0.282	-0.296	-0.259
		(-3.05)	(-3.19)	(-3.00)	(-2.93)	(-2.76)	(-3.17)	(-4.13)	(-3.72)
High sanction, low benefit		-0.324	-0.387	-0.378	-0.365	-0.360	-0.363	-0.371	-0.352
		(-4.79)	(-4.27)	(-3.87)	(-3.67)	(-3.43)	(-3.75)	(-5.13)	(-4.83)
Moderate sanction, high benefit		-0.071	-0.093	-0.073	-0.081	-0.087	-0.102	-0.114	-0.084
		(-1.05)	(-1.12)	(-0.86)	(-0.94)	(-0.98)	(-1.19)	(1.63)	(-1.22)
Moderate sanction, moderate benefit		-0.098	-0.220	-0.180	-0.183	-0.176	-0.191	-0.203	-0.177
		(-1.64)	(-2.32)	(-2.10)	(-2.10)	(-1.95)	(-2.23)	(-3.05)	(-2.69)
Moderate sanction, low benefit		-0.229	-0.344	-0.320	-0.326	-0.307	-0.324	-0.315	-0.295
		(-3.81)	(-3.68)	(-3.28)	(3.27)	(-2.94)	(-3.34)	(-4.67)	(-4.35)
Low sanction, moderate benefit		0.029	0.011	-0.020	0.020	-0.020	-0.007	-0.022	0.009
		(0.39)	(0.13)	(-0.22)	(0.22)	(-0.21)	(-0.07)	(-0.28)	(0.12)
Low sanction,		-0.118	-0.178	-0.162	-0.162	-0.155	-0.169	-0.167	-0.146
		(-1.44)	(-1.67)	(-1.50)	(-1.45)	(-1.37)	(-1.55)	(-2.07)	(-1.79)
Adjusted R-squared	0.160	0.449	0.446	0.458	0.434	0.423	0.443	0.494	0.471

Table B.5.B

Determinants of State Variation in the Postreform Period: Dependent Variable—Change in Level of Welfare Recipiency Rate, August 1996 to June 2000

(t-statistics in parentheses)

Independent Variables	Specification 1	2	3	4	5	6	7	8	9
Economic Factors									
Unemployment rate (av. (9/95–8/96) – av. (4/98–6/00))	2.978	6.446		5.992	4.342	3.012	1.301	0.669	3.736
	(0.83)	(2.46)		(1.61)	(1.12)	(0.71)	(0.36)	(0.22)	(1.14)
20th percentile wage (1996–2000)	23.106	19.158		18.345		8.841			
	(2.87)	(2.66)		(2.23)		(0.95)			
Unemployment rate (1996)						−5.071	−6.385	−6.330	
						(−1.97)	(−2.98)	(−3.14)	
20th percentile wage (1996)						0.651			
						(0.18)			
Demographic Factors									
Nonmarital birth rate (av. (1992–1996))	0.144		−0.527	−0.180	−0.397	0.409	0.477	0.626	−0.153
	(0.33)		(−1.15)	(−0.39)	(−0.84)	(0.74)	(0.90)	(1.53)	(−0.42)
% adults not citizen (FFY 1996)	−0.049		−0.794	−0.721	−0.884	−0.668	−0.736	−0.347	−0.450
	(−0.13)		(−1.58)	(−1.49)	(−1.74)	(−1.42)	(−1.61)	(−1.17)	(−1.38)
% adults 0–9 years of schooling (FFY 1996)	−0.644		−0.128	−0.260	−0.068	−0.097	−0.013		
	(−1.81)		(−0.31)	(−0.64)	(−0.16)	(−0.23)	(−0.03)		
% with 3 or more children (FFY 1996)	−1.343		−1.920	−1.546	−1.888	−1.495	−1.633	−0.962	−0.941
	(−1.89)		(−2.45)	(−2.05)	(−2.41)	(−2.05)	(−2.32)	(−1.81)	(−1.59)
% with child aged 0–2 (FFY 1996)	−0.038		1.332	0.532	1.086	0.391	0.522	0.519	1.002
	(−0.06)		(1.95)	(0.74)	(1.52)	(0.54)	(0.78)	(0.83)	(1.49)
% black case head (FFY 1996)	−0.022		0.141	0.131	0.166	0.072	0.080		
	(−0.19)		(1.07)	(1.04)	(1.25)	(0.56)	(0.65)		

Table B.5.B (continued)

Independent Variables	Specification								
	1	2	3	4	5	6	7	8	9
% Hispanic case head (FFY 1996)	0.097 (0.52)		0.268 (1.23)	0.326 (1.51)	0.347 (1.52)	0.300 (1.40)	0.312 (1.52)		
% Asian case head (FFY 1996)	0.164 (0.82)		0.250 (1.22)	0.179 (0.92)	0.241 (1.18)	0.202 (1.05)	0.237 (1.29)		
% Native American case head (FFY 1996)	0.278 (1.33)		0.340 (1.53)	0.285 (1.33)	0.287 (1.27)	0.200 (0.95)	0.189 (0.92)		
Policy Factors									
High sanction, high benefit		−9.118 (−0.77)	−6.305 (−0.46)	−11.18 (−0.85)	−10.33 (−0.74)	−15.22 (−1.18)	−15.77 (−1.25)	−16.39 (−1.42)	−8.725 (−0.70)
High sanction, moderate benefit		−6.741 (−1.16)	−11.49 (−1.38)	−13.85 (−1.72)	−13.77 (−1.61)	−15.95 (−1.90)	−17.16 (−2.20)	−16.70 (−2.57)	−10.234 (−1.49)
High sanction, low benefit		−11.84 (−1.92)	−12.16 (−1.39)	−18.02 (−2.01)	−16.29 (−1.72)	−16.32 (−1.78)	−16.24 (1.91)	−15.11 (−2.31)	−11.957 (−1.66)
Moderate sanction, high benefit		4.619 (0.75)	−1.485 (−0.19)	−2.566 (−0.33)	−3.682 (−0.45)	−6.323 (−0.81)	−7.678 (−1.03)	−4.476 (−0.71)	0.669 (0.10)
Moderate sanction, moderate benefit		0.780 (0.14)	−7.363 (−0.91)	−9.151 (−1.17)	−9.253 (−1.15)	−10.10 (−1.28)	−11.13 (−1.48)	−7.877 (−1.31)	−3.406 (−0.52)
Moderate sanction, low benefit		−9.906 (−1.81)	−15.79 (−1.75)	−18.41 (−2.06)	−19.19 (2.02)	−18.18 (−1.99)	−19.34 (−2.27)	−16.29 (−2.66)	−12.761 (−1.91)
Low sanction, moderate benefit		8.947 (1.30)	12.276 (1.47)	5.435 (0.66)	10.627 (1.26)	4.254 (0.52)	5.673 (0.74)	4.862 (0.68)	10.320 (1.34)
Low sanction, low benefit		−5.263 (−0.71)	−6.931 (−0.67)	−10.07 (−1.01)	−9.926 (−0.94)	−10.78 (−1.09)	−11.64 (−1.22)	−9.848 (−1.34)	−6.145 (−0.76)
Adjusted R-squared	0.161	0.250	0.151	0.254	0.158	0.276	0.302	0.317	0.154

evolution of caseloads (such as implemented by Figlio and Ziliak, 1999). However, even though our strategy does not use a time-series model, it does recognize the role of dynamic relationships linking economic conditions and caseload trends. Empirical specifications model the evolution of caseloads as depending on the values of economic variables averaged over a fixed period of time before caseload values are measured. Consequently, our estimated equations implicitly presume that a distributed lag relationship links economic variables and caseload measures, with the distributed lag represented by an equally weighted series of previous values truncated after a particular length. Such a formulation acknowledges that unemployment and wages can be extremely volatile. A one-month increase in the unemployment rate may have little long-term effect on welfare recipiency, especially given the seasonal nature of unemployment rates. On the other hand, an extended period of high unemployment could lead to persistently high welfare recipiency, even after the economy improves. The specifications shown in these tables use an averaged one-year lag; we considered differences in average unemployment rates over the previous 6, 12, 18, 24, and 30 months at the beginning and end of the period. Our results were not sensitive to the length of the averaging period.

Bibliography

Blank, Rebecca, "What Causes Public Assistance Caseloads to Grow?" *NBER Working Paper Series*, No. 6343, National Bureau of Economic Research, Boston, Massachusetts, 1997.

Blank, Rebecca, and Geoffrey Wallace, "What Goes Up Must Come Down? Explaining Recent Changes in Public Assistance Caseloads," in Sheldon Danziger, ed., *Economic Conditions and Welfare Reform,* Upjohn Institute for Employment Research, Kalamazoo, Michigan, 1999.

Boehnen, Elizabeth, and Thomas Corbett, "Welfare Waivers: Some Salient Trends," *Focus,* Vol. 18, No. 1, 1996, pp. 34–37.

Council of Economic Advisors (CEA), *Technical Report: Explaining the Decline in Welfare Receipt, 1993–1996,* The White House, Washington, D.C., 1997, available at http://www.whitehouse.gov/ WH/EOP/CEA/Welfare/Technical_Report.html.

Council of Economic Advisors (CEA), *Technical Report: The Effects of Welfare Policy and the Economic Expansion on Welfare Caseloads: An Update,* The White House, Washington, D.C., 1999, available at http://www.whitehouse.gov/WH/EOP/CEA/html/welfare/techv2. html.

Figlio, David, and James Ziliak, "Welfare Reform, the Business Cycle, and the Decline in AFDC Caseloads," in Sheldon Danziger, ed., *Economic Conditions and Welfare Reform,* Upjohn Institute for Employment Research, Kalamazoo, Michigan, 1999.

Lewin Group, *Determinants of AFDC Caseload Growth,* Report prepared for the Office of the Assistant Secretary for Planning and Evaluation, U.S. Department of Health and Human Services, 1997, available at http://aspe.hhs.gov/hsp/isp/afdcgrow/front.htm.

MaCurdy, Thomas, David Mancuso, and Margaret O'Brien-Strain, *The Rise and Fall of California's Welfare Caseload: Types and Regions, 1980–1999,* Public Policy Institute of California, San Francisco, California, 2000.

Martini, Alberto, and Michael Wiseman, *Explaining the Recent Decline in Welfare Caseloads: Is the Council of Economic Advisors Right?* The Urban Institute, Washington, D.C., 1997, available at http://www.urban.org/welfare/cea.htm.

Mayer, Susan E., "Why Welfare Caseloads Fluctuate: A Review of Research on AFDC, SSI, and the Food Stamps Program," *JCPR Working Paper 166,* 04-01-2000, available at http://www.jcpr.org/wp/WPprofile.cfm?ID=173.

Rector, Robert, and Sarah E. Youssef, *The Determinants of Welfare Caseload Decline: A Report of the Heritage Center for Data Analysis.* The Heritage Foundation, Washington, D.C., 1999, available at http://www.heritage.org/library/cda/cda99-04.html.

State Policy Documentation Project, available at http://www.spdp.org, a joint project of the Center for Law and Social Policy and the Center on Budget and Policy Priorities.

U.S. Department of Health and Human Services, *Characteristics and Financial Circumstances of AFDC Recipients FY1996*, available at http://www.acf.dhhs.gov/programs/ofa/cfc_fy96.htm.

U.S. Department of Health and Human Services, *TANF Program Second Annual Report to Congress*, August 1999.

U.S. Department of Health and Human Services, *TANF Program Third Annual Report to Congress*, August 2000.

Wallace, Geoffrey, and Rebecca Blank, 1999, "What Goes Up Must Come Down? Explaining Recent Changes in Public Assistance Caseloads," Paper prepared for the Welfare Reform and the Macroeconomy Conference, sponsored by the Joint Center for Poverty Research.

About the Authors

THOMAS E. MACURDY

Thomas MaCurdy is an adjunct fellow at PPIC, a professor of economics at Stanford University, and a senior fellow at the Hoover Institution. His principal research explores topics in the areas of income transfer programs, human resources, and labor markets. His recent studies investigate the consequences of governmental policies underlying welfare programs, unemployment compensation, Social Security, Medicare, Medicaid, and various forms of public assistance for low-income populations. He holds an A.B. from the University of Washington and a Ph.D. in economics from the University of Chicago.

DAVID C. MANCUSO

David Mancuso is a research associate at The SPHERE Institute. He is currently working on a range of projects related to welfare reform. Before joining SPHERE, he worked at the Legislative Analyst's Office, where he was the lead analyst in the areas of child support enforcement, child welfare services, and foster care. He holds a B.A. in economics from California State University at Fullerton and a Ph.D. in economics from Stanford University.

MARGARET O'BRIEN-STRAIN

Margaret O'Brien-Strain is a research fellow at PPIC and a research associate at The SPHERE Institute. She is interested in a broad range of public assistance questions and has written about child care, the minimum wage, the Earned Income Tax Credit, immigrants' use of welfare, the combined effects of public assistance programs, and welfare reform in California. She holds a B.A. in economics from Swarthmore College and a Ph.D. in economics from Stanford.

Other Related PPIC Publications

Employers and Welfare Recipients: The Effects of Welfare Reform in the Workplace
Harry J. Holzer, Michael A. Stoll

The Basic Skills of Welfare Recipients: Implications for Welfare Reform
Hans P. Johnson, Sonya M. Tafoya

The Rise and Fall of California's Welfare Caseload: Types and Regions, 1980–1999
Thomas MaCurdy, David Mancuso, Margaret O'Brien-Strain

Reform Reversed? The Restoration of Welfare Benefits to Immigrants in California
Thomas MaCurdy, Margaret O'Brien-Strain

Who Will Be Affected by Welfare Reform in California?
Thomas MaCurdy, Margaret O'Brien-Strain

Expensive Children in Poor Families: The Intersection of Childhood Disabilities and Welfare
Marcia K. Meyers, Henry E. Brady, Eva Y. Seto

Welfare Reform: A Primer in 12 Questions
Eugene Smolensky, Eirik Evenhouse, Siobhán Reilly

PPIC publications may be ordered by phone or from our website
(800) 232-5343 [mainland U.S.]
(415) 291-4400 [Canada, Hawaii, overseas]
www.ppic.org